Overcoming Anxiety

Reassuring ways to break free from stress and worry and lead a calmer life

Gill Hasson

CAPSTONE

This edition first published 2016

© 2016 Gill Hasson

Registered office
John Wiley & Sons Ltd, The Atrium, Southern Gate, Chichester, West Sussex, PO19 8SQ, United Kingdom

For details of our global editorial offices, for customer services and for information about how to apply for permission to reuse the copyright material in this book please see our website at www.wiley.com.

The right of the author to be identified as the author of this work has been asserted in accordan

Limit of Liability/Disclaimer of Warranty: While the publisher and author have used their best efforts in preparing this book, they make no representations or warranties with respect to the accuracy or completeness of the contents of this book and specifically disclaim any implied warranties of merchantability or fitness for a particular purpose. It is sold on the understanding that the publisher is not engaged in rendering professional services and neither the publisher nor the author shall be liable for damages arising herefrom. If professional advice or other expert assistance is required, the services of a competent professional should be sought.

Library of Congress Cataloging-in-Publication Data

Hasson, Gill, author.
  Overcoming anxiety : reassuring ways to break free from stress and worry and lead a calmer life / Gill Hasson.
    pages cm
  Includes index.
  ISBN 978-0-85708-630-3 (pbk.)
  1. Anxiety.   2. Stress management.   I. Title.
  BF575.A6H37 2016
  152.4'6—dc23
                                                          2015028627

A catalogue record for this book is available from the British Library.

ISBN 978-0-857-08630-3 (pbk)
ISBN 978-0-857-08632-7 (ebk)   ISBN 978-0-857-08631-0 (ebk)

Cover design: Wiley

Set in Sabon LT Std 11/14 by Aptara Inc., New Delhi, India

Printed in Great Britain by TJ International Ltd, Padstow, Cornwall, UK

Contents

Thanks, Marianne

Introduction
The Age of Anxiety

'A horrible dread at the pit of my stomach ... a sense of the insecurity of life.'

William James Hall

Over the last few years, I've learnt a lot about anxiety from people who come on the personal development courses and workshops I run. Increasingly, it seems that more and more people are struggling with anxiety; they describe how – in varying degrees – anxiety has affected and disrupted their lives.

Anxiety affects all of us in one way or another. You don't have to be diagnosed with an anxiety disorder to feel its intrusive, debilitating effects.

I grew up with anxiety – my Mum has been anxious all her life. There was always something she was anxious about. As soon as one anxiety was over, another would take its place. My Dad, sister and I managed Mum and her anxiety as best we could.

Fortunately, I haven't inherited my mother's persistent anxiety, but in my 20s and 30s I suffered from panic attacks. They seemed to come from nowhere. They also went away for no apparent reason. It wasn't until they went away that I even knew there was a name for them.

The Mental Health Foundation (the UK's leading mental health research, policy and service improvement charity) suggests that anxiety is one of the most prevalent mental health problems in the UK and elsewhere, yet it is still under-reported, under-diagnosed and under-treated.

A survey of 2,330 people in the UK carried out in 2014 by YouGov for the Mental Health Foundation revealed that almost one in five people feel anxious 'nearly all of the time' or 'a lot of the time'.

The Mental Health Foundation's report 'Living with Anxiety' showed that worries concerning financial issues, the welfare of children and family members, and work issues are the main factors contributing to high levels of anxiety in everyday life.

The report also highlighted the following findings:

Who gets anxious:
- Women are more likely to feel anxious than men.
- Students, young people and people not in employment are more likely to feel anxious all of the time or a lot of the time.
- Just under half of people get more anxious these days than they used to and believe that anxiety has stopped them from doing things in their life.

What people get anxious about:
- Financial issues are a cause of anxiety for half of people, but this is less likely to be the case for older people.
- Women and older people are more likely to feel anxious about the welfare of loved ones.
- Four in every ten employed people experience anxiety about their work.
- Around a fifth of people who are anxious have a fear of unemployment.
- Younger people are much more likely to feel anxious about personal relationships.
- Older people are more likely to be anxious about growing old, the death of a loved one and their own death.
- The youngest people surveyed (aged 18–24) were twice as likely to be anxious about being alone than the oldest people (aged over 55 years).

How people cope with anxiety:
- Fewer than one in ten people have sought help from their doctor to deal with anxiety, although those who feel anxious more frequently are much more likely to do this.
- The most commonly used coping strategies are talking to a friend, going for a walk and physical exercise.
- Comfort eating is used by a quarter of people to cope with feelings of anxiety; women and young people are more likely to use this as a way of coping.
- A third of the students in the survey said they cope by 'hiding themselves away from the world'.

- People who are unemployed are more likely to use coping strategies that are potentially harmful, such as alcohol and cigarettes.

Attitudes towards anxiety:
- More than a quarter of people felt that feeling anxious was a sign of not being able to cope.
- But 50% disagreed and nearly three-quarters (74%) of people said anxiety was not something to be ashamed of.

'The Age of Anxiety' appears to be defined by the pressures and uncertainties of modern life. However, the Mental Health Foundation's report concludes that 'anxiety stems as much from concern for family, friends and relationships as it does from the demands of the outside world.' The bottom line is that people can experience anxiety, and anxiety disorders, related to just about anything.

Everyone gets nervous or anxious from time to time – when speaking in public, for instance, or when going through financial difficulty. For some people, however, anxiety becomes so frequent, or so forceful, that it begins to take over their lives.

The majority of anxiety sufferers are able to function on a day-to-day basis – albeit with difficulty. But it *is* possible to worry so much that it starts to have a noticeable impact on your daily life.

Anxiety can make you feel on edge, irritable and unable to relax or concentrate. The way you think can be affected: if you fear that the worst is going to happen, you may start to see everything negatively and become very pessimistic. You may feel the need to frequently seek the reassurance of others. You may experience physical symptoms – headaches and nausea, for example.

To cope with these feelings and sensations, you may turn to smoking or drinking too much, or misusing drugs. You may hold on to relationships that either encourage your anxious outlook or help you avoid situations you find distressing – and so stop you dealing with what's worrying you.

You may withdraw from social contact and also find going to work difficult and stressful; you may take time off sick.

If your anxiety is severe, you may find it difficult to hold down a job, develop or maintain good relationships. Sleep problems may make your anxious feelings even worse and reduce your ability to cope.

For some people, anxiety becomes so overwhelming that it takes over their lives and can cause long-term mental health problems.

Whether you have occasional anxiety or a diagnosable disorder, the good news is that you can take effective and straightforward steps every day to manage and minimize your anxiety.

Things *can* be changed for the better; there's plenty you can do to understand and help yourself. This book will show you how.

Some people find it really helpful to understand what anxiety is; others just want to know what to do about it – they want advice, tips and techniques. This book does both.

The chapters in Part 1 explain exactly what anxiety is and how it can present itself – as generalized anxiety disorder, as panic attacks, phobias, OCD and/or IBS.

You will learn that anxiety manifests itself in three different ways: in the way you think, how you physically feel and the way you behave. Part 1 also explains how your thoughts, feelings and behaviour affect each other. You will also be encouraged to question and challenge negative and anxious thoughts, as well as to learn how to replace negative thoughts with more helpful, realistic ways of thinking.

In Part 2, Chapters 4 and 5 explain how to manage the cognitive aspect of anxiety: your thoughts, beliefs and expectations. Chapter 5 introduces you to ways you can use mindfulness to manage anxiety.

It can, though, feel impossible to think clearly when you're flooded with anxiety. You may need to calm down physically first. Chapter 6 explains ways that you can manage the physical feelings that come with anxiety.

Chapter 7 encourages you to focus on what you can change, rather than aspects of the situation that are beyond your control. You will learn how to find one small step you can take now and discover that once you start *doing* something – something constructive – you may feel less worried because you are moving beyond worry and doubt and doing something about it.

You will also learn how to identify activities that you can turn to when you want to switch off from worrying; something that you can dip into for ten minutes or immerse yourself in for an hour. Something that keeps you focused and engaged, that brings your complete attention to the present experience.

In Chapter 8 you will read about the role of courage, confidence and self-esteem in relation to managing anxiety. There are plenty of ideas, tips and techniques to help you assert yourself so that you are less anxious about dealing with other people.

Finally, Chapter 9 looks at the importance of reaching out to and connecting with other people. It explains what friends and family need to know, what you can ask them to do and how they can help. This final chapter also introduces the idea that other people in your life, despite their good intentions, might, without realizing it, be enabling and supporting your anxiety.

You will find some other useful support and general resources at the back of the book.

Throughout the book, there are quotes and examples from other people who have experienced anxiety. You will read about their ways of managing and overcoming their worries, anxieties and fears in a range of situations – at work, at home and in social situations.

Also throughout the book, there are exercises, activities and tips, strategies and techniques for you to try. However, not every tip, technique or strategy works the same for everyone and every anxious experience. What is crucial is that you learn and develop a range of techniques and strategies that work for *you*. Some of the tips and techniques you pick up will bring quick results. Others – like learning to accept or change the way you think – will take time and practice.

You've got to work at it to identify ways to manage your anxiety that work for you – and keep at it. Yes, it can be tedious, boring and hard work, but anxiety can be those things too. Learning to manage anxiety is much more positive than being controlled by anxiety!

PART ONE

Understanding Anxiety

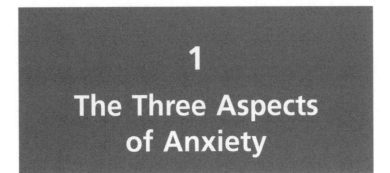

1
The Three Aspects
of Anxiety

Who hasn't, at one time or another, been worried or anxious?

We've all experienced doubts, fears and worries; most of us have experienced feeling tense, uncertain and even fearful at the thought of speaking to a group or sitting an exam, having an operation, attending an interview or starting a new job.

Maybe right now you're worried about a forthcoming social event or driving somewhere new on your own. Perhaps you get anxious when your partner or teenager is late home. If everything goes well – your partner or teenager arrives home, the social event or the journey has been and gone – the anxiety will go with it, but until it is over, the hours, days or weeks leading up to it can be very difficult.

Perhaps you're worried about losing your job or something dreadful happening to your partner or children. You may be anxious about events that feel like they're beyond your control: being attacked, being made redundant or never being able to own your own home. Perhaps you fret about global warming or getting cancer.

Whatever it is that's worrying you and making you anxious, it can have an effect on both your body and your mind. Anxiety can leave you feeling uncomfortable or even physically unwell. It can be an annoying distraction or it can leave you unable to think about anything else whatsoever.

Anxiety can erode your confidence and self-esteem, affect your relationships and friendships and impair your ability to study and work. If, for whatever reason, you experience prolonged or intense anxiety, you may find it difficult to deal with in your everyday life; you may feel powerless and out of control.

'Sometimes, anxiety takes over my life – I find myself worrying about everything, even small things like my son forgetting his PE kit become an overwhelming concern.'

After a while, you may start to fear the symptoms of anxiety and this can set up a vicious circle. You may be anxious because you dread the feelings of anxiety, but then you experience those symptoms because you're having anxious thoughts. You feel that something bad will or might happen and you don't know how or if you will be able to cope.

Anxiety is the anticipation of trouble, misfortune or adversity, difficulties or disaster. If you haven't any experience of an event or situation, you may be anxious about what could happen or how you will cope with it. But if you *have* experienced a particular situation and you found it difficult or distressing in some way, you may be anxious about facing a similar situation again in case it brings up the same challenges and difficulties.

Is there a difference between anxiety and fear, worry and doubt? Doubt happens when you feel uncertain about something: you think it's unlikely that something will turn out well. Worry concerns feelings of unease and feeling troubled. *Fear* is a reaction to *immediate* danger – your car going into a skid, for example, or a child running into the road – whereas anxiety involves a response to something farther away in the future: something that's going to happen later today, tomorrow, next week and so on. It could be, for example, an interview, a plane flight or speaking up at a meeting. You could be feeling anxious but you don't know what exactly you're anxious about.

Whether it's fear, anxiety, worry or doubt, the feelings are very much the same. Why? Why does anxiety so often have such a debilitating effect? It helps to understand what, exactly, anxiety is.

Just like fear, worry and doubt, anxiety is an emotion. Emotions cause us to feel, think and act in different ways: they can cause us to do something or avoid doing something.

All emotions, including anxiety, have a positive intent: worrying and feeling anxious about doing well before an exam or giving a presentation, for example, can prompt you to prepare well and keep you alert and focused.

However, like all other emotions, anxiety becomes a problem if, instead of prompting you to respond in a way that's helpful, it overwhelms or paralyses you. In the example of exams, if anxiety takes over, your stomach may be in knots, your heart thumps and negative thoughts can dominate your mind. Your ability to revise, think straight and concentrate suffers.

It's not, though, just how and what you think that can make you anxious. Again, just like all other emotions, anxiety has three parts: physical feelings, thoughts and behaviour. Let's look at each of these aspects more closely.

Physical aspect

This part of anxiety involves the physical changes that occur in your body – the internal bodily changes you experience.

Some of the most common physical symptoms of anxiety are:

- Muscle tension, which can cause headaches, tension in your jaw, neck and shoulder pain or tightness in your throat and chest.
- Rapid breathing, which may make you feel weak, light-headed and shaky, and may give you pins and needles in your fingers and toes.
- Rising blood pressure, which can make you more aware of a pounding heart.
- A rush of hormones, which can give you hot flushes and make you sweat.

- Changes in the blood supply to your digestive system, which may cause 'butterflies', nausea and sickness.
- Frequent visits to the loo.

Anxiety can go undiagnosed – especially if it presents as a physical problem. Stomach problems, for example – a queasy tummy, feelings of nausea and/or a frequent, urgent need to use the loo – can often be the result of feeling anxious about a forthcoming event, but may not be recognized as such.

Although we each have different thoughts when we are anxious, we all have very similar *physical* responses. Regardless of age, race or gender, when we are stressed, anxious or frightened our bodies release hormones which spread to different parts of the body. Adrenaline causes your heart to beat faster to carry blood where it's most needed. You breathe more rapidly to provide the extra oxygen required for energy. You sweat to prevent overheating. Your digestive system slows down to allow more blood to be sent to your muscles. Your senses become heightened and your brain is on full alert.

These changes help your body to take action to protect you in a dangerous situation, either by running away or fighting. This is known as the 'fight or flight' reflex. Once the danger has passed, other hormones are released, which may cause you to tremble and feel weak as your muscles start to relax.

This response is useful for protecting you against physical dangers – a runaway car or a falling tree, for example – but if there is no physical threat and you don't need to run away or fight, the effects of adrenaline subside more slowly and you may go on feeling agitated for a long time.

'The feeling of having in the middle of my body a ball of wool that quickly winds itself up, its innumerable threads pulling from the surface of my body to itself.'

Franz Kafka

Interestingly, two very different emotions – anxiety and excitement – provoke the same physical response: rapid breathing and a pounding heart. In that case, what determines whether what you feel is happy or anxious? Your thoughts.

Cognitive aspect

Your thoughts – your beliefs, perceptions and interpretations of a forthcoming event – are the cognitive aspect of anxiety.

Different people may have different thoughts about a situation. For example, in the case of sitting an exam, one person might be thinking, 'I don't know if I can do this. I might be hopeless. I could fail.' But another person's thoughts might be, 'What if I forget everything I revised? Supposing they don't ask questions related to the topics I've revised?' Often, added to your thoughts and concerns about a situation are the thoughts you might have about how you'll feel or behave once you're in that situation. You might think that you will:

- Lose control or go 'mad';
- Have a heart attack, be sick, faint or be incontinent;

- Be unable to stop thinking that people are looking at you and know you're anxious;
- Feel like things are speeding up/slowing down and that you'll be detached from your environment and the people in it;
- Want to run away and escape from the situation.

When your anxiety is high, you don't just think, 'I don't know if I can do this. I might be hopeless. I could fail.' You know and truly believe something: 'I *can't* do this. I *will* be hopeless. I *will* fail.'

When anxiety takes hold, rather than just acknowledge what might happen, you are convinced it *will* happen. This is known as 'cognitive fusion' – when a thought becomes fused with what it refers to. You experience a thought as a fact, a reality and an inevitability.

Behavioural aspect

The behavioural part of anxiety is the things you do or don't do when you're anxious. Just as we each have differing thoughts about a situation, we each behave in different ways too.

If, for example, you were anxious before an exam, you might pace up and down the room. But someone else might sit and bite their nails as a result of their worry or anxiety. Someone else might chain smoke or chew gum.

How we each behave when we're anxious or worried depends on a variety of things, including what has triggered the anxiety, our ability to manage the situation and how the situation relates to our past experiences.

Instead of responding by doing something, your behaviour might involve *not* doing something: *avoidance* behaviour. In the example of the exam, you might actually avoid it by not turning up to sit the exam.

So, when you experience anxiety, it will be made up of these three aspects: physical, cognitive and behavioural. Imagine, for example, that you were anxious about speaking to a group of people. Here's how you might experience the anxiety:

- *Physical response:* Rapid breathing, increased pulse, stomach churning and hot flushes.
- *Cognitive response:* 'Oh no, I'll waffle on and not make myself clear and everyone will think I don't know what I'm talking about. I don't think I can do this.'
- *Behavioural response:* Biting your nails and fiddling with your pen.

There is no particular order in which the aspects of anxiety – or any other emotion – occur, but any one aspect can affect the others: how you think, feel and act are intrinsically linked.

For example, your anxious response to speaking to a group of people could begin with a *physical* reaction: rapid breathing, increased pulse, stomach churning and hot flushes. This may trigger a *behavioural* reaction: you bite your nails and fiddle with your pen. This may be immediately followed by the *thought,* 'Oh no, I'll waffle on and not make myself clear and everyone will think I don't know what I'm talking about. I don't think I can do this.'

Or you could start biting your nails and fiddling with your pen first. This could trigger a physical response: rapid breathing, increased pulse, stomach churning and hot flushes. Again, your thoughts would follow closely behind.

Or your anxious response could begin with the thought, 'Oh no, I'll waffle on and not make myself clear and everyone will think I don't know what I'm talking about. I don't think I can do this.' This thought may then trigger rapid breathing, increased pulse, stomach churning and hot flushes. You then start biting your nails and fiddling with your pen.

To understand how this interaction of thoughts, feelings and behaviours works when you're anxious, write down your own example of an event that you often feel anxious about.

Situation:

Physical response: How I physically feel

Cognitive response: My thoughts

Behavioural response: What I do or don't do

Self-sustaining nature of anxiety

Seeing anxiety in terms of thoughts, physical feelings and behaviour makes it easier to see how they are connected and how they affect you. You can also see how anxiety can be self-sustaining: one aspect can feed another. For example, the more anxious thoughts you have, the more you might experience the physical feelings: a pounding heart, sweating and feeling short of breath. This might then prompt you to resort to unhelpful behaviours, which, in turn, make it more likely you'll experience further anxiety.

You may find yourself feeling anxious about feeling anxious. This then creates a spiral of difficult thoughts, feelings and behaviour.

You might, for example, feel anxious about speaking in meetings at work. You get hot and flustered and feel nauseous at the mere thought of being asked to speak at a meeting. Then you get anxious about your anxiety showing and everyone knowing you're anxious. So you do what you can to avoid meetings. But then you become anxious that your manager thinks you have nothing to contribute and as a result you feel you must work harder in other areas of your job in order to show that you do have something to contribute. Before you know it, you're in a cycle of worry.

And if you then dread your anxiety and its symptoms – the thoughts, feelings and behaviours – you may also develop new anxieties, or find more situations causing anxiety.

'My anxiety gives me moments of panic, fear and dread. I have so many physical symptoms such as headaches, tingling in my fingers and stomach pains to the point where I think I must be ill with some terrible terminal disorder. Otherwise, why would I feel like this?'

Nature or nurture?

Are you born to be anxious or do you 'learn' to be anxious?

It could be that some people are born sensitive and pre-disposed to worry and anxiety. In his book *The Temperamental Thread: How Genes, Culture, Time and Luck Make Us Who We Are*, Harvard Professor Dr Jerome Kagan suggests that some of us display 'high-reactive' behaviour in the first few weeks and months of infancy and go on to be sensitive children and to be careful, cautious teenagers. However, for many 'high-reactive' children, as they move into adolescence, they seem to 'grow out' of being quiet, shy and timid. It just may be, though, that they've learnt to suppress or keep their worries hidden so their anxieties are not always apparent to others.

It could be, though, that you weren't born anxious but that feeling anxious could be something you *learned* early on in life. Close family members may have tended to be worried and anxious and transferred their anxiety to you. You then learned to respond in the same way.

Past stressful or traumatic experiences, such as domestic violence, abuse or bullying, can certainly contribute to anxiety. If common childhood fears, such as a fear of the dark or a fear of being left alone, weren't handled well by parents, the child may be more prone to anxiety in later life. If you had a lot of change in your life when you were young, for example, moving house and schools, being ill (or someone close to you being ill) or seeing your parents separating – all events where you may have been unsure about what was going to happen next – this might make you more prone to anxiety.

If something distressing happened to you in the past – either as a child or an adult – and you struggled to deal with your emotions at the time, you may become anxious about the possibility of similar situations happening again in case they stir up the same anxious feelings.

'I've been bullied at work on and off for a number of years and I've suffered anxiety on a daily basis.'

Some people can clearly pinpoint a cause for their anxiety: a traumatic incident, a build-up of stress or having undergone a significant life event such as losing their job, a relationship breakdown or having surgery. It could be a current situation or a number of events or cumulative events that you are finding very stressful.

However, some people don't have an identifiable cause for their anxiety.

Anxiety, then, may be triggered by one thing or several events. It could be that you were born predisposed to being anxious or that it's a result of your upbringing, your past and/or current experiences. It could be a mixture of any of these factors.

What is certain, though, is that there is a sum total of forces at work when you're anxious: thoughts, physical feelings and behaviour. And these forces, these aspects, interact with each other. Understanding this can help demystify anxiety. It can help you better understand the nature of anxiety – how and why it prompts you to feel, think and behave as you do when you're anxious.

The next step is to understand more about what can trigger anxiety and the different ways in which anxiety can present itself. Chapter 2 explains this.

In a nutshell

- Anxiety is the anticipation of trouble, misfortune or adversity, difficulties or disaster.
- Anxiety becomes a problem if, instead of prompting you to respond in a way that's helpful, it overwhelms or paralyses you.
- There are three aspects to anxiety: physical feelings, thoughts and behaviour.
  - The physical aspects help your body to take action to protect you in a dangerous situation. But if there is no real physical threat, your body may feel tense and wired for quite a long time.
  - The cognitive aspect of anxiety is your thoughts: the negative, distressing things you think and believe about what could or will happen.
  - The behavioural part of anxiety is the things you do or don't do when you're anxious.
- The three different aspects of anxiety interact with each other: any one part can trigger or feed another, which means that anxiety can be self-sustaining.

2
Understanding Your Own Anxiety

How can you tell if your everyday anxiety has crossed the line into a disorder? It's not easy. Sometimes, the symptoms of anxiety are not obviously the result of anxiety. They often develop gradually and, given that we all experience some anxiety at one time or another, it can be hard to know when it's become a real problem.

Perhaps you feel a persistent free-floating or nagging, unidentifiable sense of anxiety. Some people may experience panic attacks or develop a phobia. Others have obsessive thoughts and compulsive behaviour. The term 'anxiety' covers a whole range of disorders.

In this chapter, you can read about the most common anxiety disorders. The aim here is not to make a diagnosis of an anxiety disorder or take the place of a professional diagnosis or consultation. You may well have received a diagnosis and have been prescribed medication or another form of support – Cognitive Behavioural Therapy, for example.

Rather, the aim is to help you recognize and understand the ways in which anxiety can present itself, so that once you understand your anxiety disorder, you will better understand the ways you can help yourself – the techniques and strategies you can adopt – which are explained in the rest of this book.

Generalized Anxiety Disorder (GAD)

Generalized anxiety disorder, often known as 'chronic worrying' or a 'free-floating' anxiety, means that you feel anxious about a wide range of situations and issues over a long period – six months or more – rather than because of one specific event.

If you experience GAD then you probably feel anxious most days and probably can't remember the last time you felt calm and relaxed. You may worry about the same things that other people do – health, finances, family or work – but for you, these worries are at a different level.

Normal worry	Generalized anxiety disorder
Your worrying doesn't get in the way of your everyday activities	Worrying and anxiety disrupt your everyday life: work, responsibilities, family and social life
You can control your worries	Worries and anxious thoughts take over and feel uncontrollable
Worrying and anxious thoughts are unpleasant and even upsetting but don't cause significant distress	You feel disturbed and distressed by your worries and anxious thoughts

Your worries focus on a small number of specific issues and concerns	You worry about anything and everything, and tend to expect the worst
Your bouts of worrying last for only a short time period	You've been worrying almost every day for at least six months

'My worries just seem to hum along in the background. I feel restless and on edge. I'm unable to relax. Sometimes I have a sense of dread or of *impending doom*.'

Physical symptoms

Physical symptoms include dizziness, tiredness, muscle aches and tension, trembling or shaking, palpitations, shortness of breath, nausea, diarrhoea, headache, pins and needles, feeling hot and cold, loss of appetite and difficulty sleeping.

Cognitive symptoms

You worry about all sorts of things and have a tendency to think the worst. Often, you may not be able to identify what you are feeling anxious about. Not knowing why you are anxious can add to the problem, as you may worry that there will be no solution. It feels uncontrollable. Sometimes just the thought of getting through the day produces anxiety.

Behavioural symptoms

You probably find it difficult to relax, either with other people or when you're on your own, and you may struggle to focus and concentrate. You may seek reassurance from other people and often postpone or cancel things because you feel overwhelmed.

'My worrying feels uncontrollable; whatever it is I'm worried about, no sooner is it resolved than another worry pops up.'

Sometimes, if the anxiety overwhelms you, you may experience a panic attack.

Panic attacks

A panic attack is an exaggeration of your body's normal response to fear, stress or excitement. There is a rush of intense psychological and physical symptoms. These vary from person to person.

'I remember the first time I had a panic attack: I was feeling a little apprehensive about being in a room with so many people. It didn't seem like a big deal; although it was very crowded, I didn't feel freaked out. Suddenly, though, I felt a wave of intense heat. I then felt very cold. But then I was hot again. I felt very weak and had to sit down so that I didn't fall down. My heart was hammering and I was breathing very rapidly. My face had lost all colour. I had no idea what was happening.

I continued feeling this way for about 15 minutes then the symptoms slowly subsided. I felt completely drained.'

Physical symptoms

Most of the symptoms of a panic attack are physical, and many times these symptoms are so severe that people think they're having a heart attack. You may experience a pounding and/or irregular heartbeat, feeling faint, sweating, nausea, chest pains, breathing discomfort, shortness of breath, a choking sensation, feelings of losing control, trembling body and shaky limbs.

As your body tries to take in more oxygen, your breathing increases. Your body releases hormones such as adrenaline, causing your heart to beat faster and your muscles to tense up.

These physical symptoms are very unpleasant and the accompanying psychological thoughts of terror can make a panic attack a pretty frightening experience.

> 'I'm walking to pick up the children from school, then my heart's hammering as if it will explode, my vision is blurred and my hands are sweating.'

You may also be woken up by a panic attack. Night-time attacks happen when, due to anxiety, your brain is on 'high alert.' It detects small changes in your body which it then interprets as danger signals.

Cognitive symptoms
You may be thinking 'Oh my God. Oh my God' over and over again and experience an overwhelming sense of terror, fear or a sense of unreality, as if you're detached from the world around you. Possibly, you think that you are going mad, having a heart attack and are going to die.

Behavioural symptoms
You will probably need to sit or lie down. You might find yourself frozen to the spot but will want to get away and escape. If you often experience panic attacks, you may

start avoiding more and more situations for fear of experiencing a panic attack in that situation.

Panic attacks come on very quickly, with most panic attacks lasting for between 5 and 20 minutes. Some people may experience more than one attack after another or a high level of anxiety after the initial attack.

You may have one or two panic attacks and never experience another, or they may occur every couple of weeks or more than once a week. For some people a panic attack can come without warning and strike at random. You start to dread the next attack and quickly enter into a cycle of living in fear of fear.

Eventually, this can lead to anticipatory anxiety, which stems from a fear of having future panic attacks. This 'fear of fear' is present most of the time and can be extremely disabling. It may also lead to phobic avoidance: you begin to avoid certain situations or environments that you think may have caused a previous panic attack. Or you may avoid places where escape would be difficult or help would be unavailable if you had a panic attack.

Phobias

Phobias can restrict your day-to-day life and cause you considerable distress and misery.

Physical symptoms
As well as a racing heart, chest pain and tightness, feeling dizzy or light-headed, you may express and show signs of

fear or discomfort: sweating, trembling, breathing rapidly and so on.

Cognitive symptoms
You may find yourself overwhelmed by thoughts that you are going to pass out or die and that you must escape. Although you might tell yourself that you're overreacting, it has little or no effect.

Behavioural symptoms
You could feel the need to organize your life around avoiding whatever it is that's causing the anxiety. You will avoid direct contact with the objects or situations and may even avoid any mention or depiction of them.

Phobias may be specific and simple or they can be complex.

Specific (simple) phobias are unreasonable or irrational fears over specific objects or situations. Simple phobias often develop in childhood or adolescence and for many people they will lessen as they get older.

Here's how 16-year-old Charlie describes his phobia of metal:

> 'I don't know why but I don't like metal things. I don't like coins, keys, small earrings on women. For some reason, I don't mind my own keys. I don't like the feel of metal.
>
> And I don't like metal with metal – my Mum has her keys with a small metal charm on her keyring. Just hearing people talking about these things...my brother used to tease me that he was going to put one hundred pennies in my bed.

When I buy something in a shop I'd rather not have the change. In fact, before I buy an item I look for a charity box on the counter to put the change into. I'm pleased that 1ps and 2ps are being phased out. I used not to be able to see money on a table – I'd not go into the room. As I've got older, I don't feel so strongly or fearful though.'

Complex phobias can have a more disruptive impact on your life than specific, simple phobias. They tend to develop when you are an adult. Two of the most common complex phobias are social phobia and agoraphobia.

'It stops me living my life. Things that other people do easily, without any thought, become a huge ordeal for me.'

Social phobia
Many of us find social situations difficult, or feel shy or awkward in certain situations. That's normal. However, if you have social phobia (also called social anxiety), you will feel a sense of actual fear in social situations. Not only parties and social gatherings but simple everyday activities, such as shopping or speaking on the phone, can trigger anxiety for you.

You may be excessively self-conscious, be anxious about how you look, fear being the centre of attention, worry what others think of you and worry that they'll notice that you're anxious. You could be anxious about other people's motives, intentions, thoughts, what they might say or be saying.

'The longer I've got to think about an upcoming social event, the more time I've got to worry and the worse it is.

It spoils my week leading up to it as it takes over my thoughts. I'll worry excessively about it. It depresses me. By the time the event comes around, I feel shaky, hot, sweaty. I struggle to find the right words to say and my mind goes blank. I'm embarrassed that people are aware of this.'

Physical symptoms

Being around other people or just the thought of being with others might get your heart racing and increase your breathing rate. When you are with other people, you may blush, feel tearful, shake and sweat or simply fear that it might show that you're experiencing these things. You could feel chest pain and tightness, feel nauseous, dizzy or light-headed.

Cognitive symptoms

Fears of feeling humiliated, embarrassed and unable to take part in conversation and/or being 'found out' as a fake or incompetent can dominate your thoughts.

You could spend hours in turmoil trying to talk yourself into facing the 'ordeal' of even the simplest of social situations such as coffee with a friend.

Behavioural symptoms

You may avoid social contact completely or at least as much as you possibly can. This can make everyday life difficult: going to work, using public transport, going to the shops, meeting friends for coffee or a meal or joining in with other people who share the same interests. You might avoid getting into conversation and/or avoid eating or drinking with other people.

Having a social phobia can make it difficult to seek support, particularly if you feel unable to speak on the phone or meet with people who could help you.

'I can't answer the phone or even open letters or read emails. The thought of doing these things makes me panic.'

Agoraphobia
Although agoraphobia is usually thought of as a fear of open spaces, it's more complex than that. (The word agoraphobia is derived from Greek words which translate as 'fear of the marketplace.')

The essential characteristic of agoraphobia is that you will feel anxious about being in places or situations that it would be difficult or embarrassing to get out of, or where you might not be able to get help if the anxiety completely overwhelmed you. Being in a crowd of people, going to the shops, travelling by car, bus, train or plane, being on a bridge or in a lift, for example, may all be situations that you get anxious about. Your fear will also be more intense if getting away is difficult.

'I've suffered from panic disorder since I was 14. Recently, my symptoms – shortness of breath, sweating, trembling, blurred vision, nausea – have overwhelmed me and I've left my course at university. I just stay at home all day. I just can't do anything. I feel like my life is on hold.'

Physical symptoms
You probably experience many of the physical symptoms that come with other anxiety disorders – shortness of breath, thumping heartbeat, trembling, blurred vision, nausea and so on.

Cognitive symptoms
You may find the thought of leaving the house stressful, but also fear being alone inside or outside the home. If you do feel stuck in a situation, your only thought could be, 'I've got to get out; I've got to get out.'

Behavioural symptoms
If you develop agoraphobia, you probably avoid crowded places such as pubs, bars, cafés and restaurants. You will stay away from shops and public attractions: museums, theatres, parks and so on. You might also find cars, aeroplanes, subways and other forms of travel too much to manage.

Agoraphobia often develops as a complication of panic disorder. It may arise as a result of associating panic attacks with the places or situations where the panic attack occurred and then wanting to avoid those places in future.

Obsessive Compulsive Disorder (OCD)

Obsessive Compulsive Disorder (OCD) is an anxiety-related condition where a person experiences frequent intrusive, obsessive thoughts and compulsive behaviour.

'I don't feel I have a choice. I have to do them, these behaviours. Everything I do feels so controlled by it. If I don't go back up the stairs twice, my husband will die in an accident at work.

If I don't check all the doors and windows five times once I get home from work then someone will definitely be able to break in. I know it's not rational and I try to hide it. Trying to hide it is so stressful though.'

The obsessive part of OCD is the unpleasant, persistent and uncontrollable thought, image, worry, fear, impulse or urge that repeatedly enters your mind. These thoughts, worries, etc. can cause feelings of unease, distress, anxiety or disgust.

The compulsive part of OCD is the repetitive behaviour or mental thought rituals that you feel you need to carry out over and over again in an attempt to relieve the anxiety caused by the obsessive thoughts. Examples of compulsions are excessive cleaning, counting, checking, measuring and repeating tasks or actions. But OCD presents itself in many guises, not just hand washing or checking locks or light switches.

You feel less anxious once you have carried out a compulsion. It is, though, possible to experience obsessive thoughts only and not feel the need to carry out a compulsion.

The physical symptoms of OCD will be similar to other anxiety disorders.

The unwanted, intrusive disturbing thoughts significantly interfere with your day-to-day life as they are very difficult to ignore. You may realize that your obsessional thoughts are irrational, but feel that the only way to relieve the anxiety caused by these thoughts is to perform compulsive behaviours, often to prevent perceived harm happening to yourself or, more often than not, to a loved one.

Irritable bowel syndrome (IBS)

IBS is a common condition that can cause stomach pain, cramps, bloating, diarrhoea and incontinence. These symptoms may be caused by a physical condition but can also be symptoms of anxiety.

> 'Mum was complaining of stomach problems for a few months. The doctor could find nothing wrong with her. It was only after she voiced her worries and fears about the hip replacement operation she was waiting for, that my sister and I realized that all those symptoms – the churning stomach, feeling queasy and nauseous and frequent trips to the loo and so on, were as a result of her anxiety about the operation.'

Even if you've not suffered from IBS, there will probably have been times when you've been very worried, nervous or anxious and experienced a churning stomach and the need to frequently visit the loo. This is your digestive system reacting to stress and anxiety; a result of the so-called 'brain–gut connection'.

In your stomach and gut, just like in your brain, you have a network consisting of millions of nerve cells (neurons) which make up your enteric nervous system. It's so complex it has been dubbed 'the second brain.'

The neurons in the stomach don't actually 'think' – analyse, rationalize and reason, etc. – in the same way as your brain does, but digestion – breaking down food and extracting the nutrients – is a complicated business, so it needs its own network of nerves to oversee it.

Although you are not conscious of your gut 'thinking,' nerve signals sent from the gut to the brain via the vagus nerve create gut reactions which can affect your emotional state and can be felt as excitement, fear, disgust or anxiety, for example.

If you get nervous, anxious or fearful, blood gets diverted from your gut to your muscles as part of the fight or flight response instigated by the brain. These changes in the blood supply to your digestive system may cause a variety of physical symptoms.

Physical symptoms
IBS can cause bouts of stomach cramps, bloating, wind, diarrhoea, constipation and nausea.

If you experience regular and persistent anxiety, it may be that your stomach is constantly bothering you.

Cognitive symptoms
Anxiety can cause your mind to focus on the physical issues that are bothering you the most, and so when your stomach is bothering you because of anxiety, your anxious thoughts about your stomach symptoms may increase.

Behavioural symptoms
If, as a result of IBS, you've ever experienced diarrhoea or incontinence, you might be anxious if you think you won't have easy access to a toilet. Again, this anxiety creates extra sensitivity in the gut, and a cycle of anxious thoughts and stomach and bowel problems is established.

Whatever the trigger, intensity or object of your anxiety, it can force changes on you that make it harder to cope with and manage.

Many people continue to live their day-to-day lives but in a difficult way. Their lives may be ruled by doubt, fear, avoidance, subterfuge, rituals and compulsions and self-medication – drinking, disordered eating and/or drugs.

In his book *The Monkey Mind*, Daniel Smith tells his own funny but sad story of his struggle to hide his extreme perspiration from his colleagues – a struggle that he 'solved' by wearing sanitary towels under his arms before any important meeting.

Smith's struggles with anxiety saw him leaving a job he loved, and he and his girlfriend separated. Even he, though, found that therapy combined with changes to his work life improved his mental health in the end. And this is what is known – anxiety might be a problem with a long lifespan, but it *is* treatable.

In a nutshell

- Sometimes, the symptoms of anxiety are not obvious as being the result of anxiety. They may develop gradually and it can be hard to know when it's become an anxiety disorder.
- Having *generalized anxiety disorder* (GAD) means that you feel anxious about a wide range of situations and issues over a long period rather than because of one specific event.

- A *panic attack* is an exaggeration of your body's normal response to fear, stress or excitement; you experience a rush of intense psychological and physical symptoms.
- *Phobias* may be specific and simple or they can be complex. Specific (simple) phobias are unreasonable or irrational fears over specific objects or situations whereas complex phobias involve a number of different, interrelated aspects.
- *Obsessive Compulsive Disorder* (OCD) is an anxiety-related condition where a person experiences frequent intrusive, obsessive thoughts and compulsive behaviour.
- *IBS* is a common condition that can cause stomach cramps, bloating and diarrhoea. These symptoms may be caused by a physical condition but can also be symptoms of anxiety.
- Whatever the trigger, intensity or object of your anxiety, it can force changes on you that make it harder to cope with and manage. It *is*, though, treatable.

3
Understanding the Way You Think

Jess is worrying about moving from Doncaster to London to start a new job. She was going to drive down but she had never done the journey by car before. Last time she drove somewhere new she got lost. Jess is feeling anxious and panicky about it: 'I'll never get there. I won't be able to sleep the night before so then I'll be too tired to think straight. I just know I'll be stressed and I'll get horribly lost.'

Julia is facing an important deadline at work. She's anxious about what will happen if she misses it: 'I should have been given more time for this. I'll be in trouble with my manager. She'll use this against me. Even if I do get it finished on time, it won't be good enough. The rest of my team will think I'm incompetent; that I'm not up to it. I'm such an idiot! I'm always making mistakes. I should have been able to do this really well and got it finished on time.'

Sal is feeling stressed because his partner may lose her job. Money is tight right now. Job opportunities are thin on the ground. Sal's worry turns into despair: 'It's not fair. What have we done to deserve this? We won't manage.

We're going to end up homeless. The kids' lives will be ruined.'

Jess's, Julia's and Sal's situations are all normal things to worry and be anxious about. They may be different situations but one thing links them: each situation is characterized by the negative thoughts accompanying them.

Negative thoughts fixate on negative outcomes. They are self-perpetuating: each thought creates another negative thought until your mind is filled with negativity. There's certainly no room for more positive, helpful ways of thinking.

How does this happen? It helps to understand how the thoughts in our minds work.

The core components of our brain are neurons: cells in the nervous system that process and transmit information. The interconnections between neurons mean that, when you think (or do) something your brain uses 'neural pathways'. It's rather like walking through a field of long grass, where each step helps to create a path.

Every time you repeat the same thought or type of thought, your brain uses the same neural pathways; each time your brain continues to use these same pathways they become stronger. Eventually, they become your mind's automatic way of thinking.

So, if we take the field of long grass analogy, each time you walk that way, you create a strong, distinct path. It becomes the easiest route to take.

Regardless of whether your thoughts and actions are positive or negative, they become a habit. This means that negative thinking patterns can become a habit. They become your normal way of thinking.

The challenge, then, is to change the way you think – to create new, helpful, positive thinking pathways. It's not easy to do this – to break a habit – but it's also never too late to start a new one!

You can make a start by being aware of your thinking patterns.

The way you think

In all of the scenarios at the beginning of this chapter, each situation is characterized by the negative thoughts that Jess, Julia and Sal have about their situations. Each of them has a habit of negative thinking. And yet none of them started out in life thinking so negatively.

Just like Jess, Julia and Sal, whatever the personality type we may have been born with, our patterns of thinking and behaving, our thoughts, expectations and beliefs have developed over the years as a result of our upbringing, environment, education, religion, class and culture.

Other people – parents, teachers, other adults and peers – encourage us to think in certain ways and to believe certain 'truths'. They also discourage us from questioning or disputing certain 'truths'.

For many of us, because we are discouraged from questioning and contradicting what we are told, we suppress the instinct to question our own thinking; to question how logical, realistic or helpful our thoughts are.

To a greater or lesser extent, we simply accept particular beliefs and ways of thinking. That's all well and good if those thoughts are helpful and constructive. It's not so good if those ways of thinking are negative and produce thoughts and feelings that are self-defeating and destructive.

Self-talk and cognitive distortions

Your thoughts can be understood as your 'self-talk' or your 'inner voice'. Your self-talk provides you with a running commentary rather like the constant text at the bottom of 24-hour news channels. This self-talk directs your thinking and shapes your beliefs and actions. It can be:

- Neutral (for example, 'I think I'll make a cup of tea');
- Positive – helpful and constructive – ('I can do this');
- Negative – critical and resigned – ('I can't do this. I'm hopeless') – the type of thinking that comes with being worried and anxious.

Self-talk isn't just mindless chatter; it has a way of creating its own reality. Telling yourself you can do something can help it happen. Telling yourself you *can't* do something can make that more likely to be true. And because your brain speaks with your own voice, it feels real and it feels true.

Thinking in negative, unhelpful ways is also known as 'cognitive distortion'. Cognitive distortions are illogical or irrational ways of thinking. They are powerful because they can easily convince you of something – that your thoughts *are* rational and true. But actually, they are unhelpful and limiting; they're not good for you.

Cognitive distortions can make you feel bad about yourself and your abilities. Take Julia's thoughts, for example, from the beginning of this chapter: 'I should have been given more time for this. I'll be in trouble with my manager. She'll use this against me. Even if I do get it finished on time, it won't be good enough. The rest of my team will think I'm incompetent; that I'm not up to it. I'm such an idiot! I'm always making mistakes. I should have been able to do this really well and got it finished on time.'

Cognitive distortions
There's a range of ways in which cognitive distortions and negative thinking habits occur. Below are some examples.

Jumping to a conclusion
This involves judging or deciding something *will* happen without considering all the facts. You anticipate that things will turn out badly, and are quite sure that your prediction is already an established fact. For example, 'I just know I'll be stressed and I'll get horribly lost.'

Catastrophizing
When you catastrophize, you expect disaster to strike, no matter what: 'We are going to end up homeless. The kids' lives will be ruined.'

Overgeneralization
In this cognitive distortion, if something bad happens once, you believe it will happen every time in similar situations. You see one difficult event as part of a never-ending pattern of defeat: 'I screwed up. I'm obviously going to screw up every time.'

Mind reading
This means that you believe you know what the other person was thinking: 'The rest of my team will think I'm incompetent; that I'm not up to it.'

Tunnel thinking
This involves paying too much attention to one or more negative details, instead of seeing the whole picture. You're unable to recognize that there are other ways of doing things or thinking about things: 'I'll never get there. I won't be able to sleep the night before, then I'll be too tired to think straight. I'll be stressed. All I can think about is getting horribly lost.'

Filtering
This is similar to tunnel thinking; you take the negative details and dwell on them exclusively while filtering out all possible positive aspects of a situation.

Polarized thinking (or black and white) thinking
With polarized thinking, things are either black or white; there are no grey areas. There's no middle ground or allowing for the complexity of people and situations. For example, you may believe 'Other people should be completely trustworthy otherwise you can't trust them at all.'

When it comes to thinking about yourself, if you fall short of perfect, you see yourself as a failure.

'Shoulds'

We all have beliefs about how we and others 'should,' 'shouldn't,' 'must,' 'mustn't,' 'ought' or 'ought not' to behave. However, thoughts that include these words create rigid, unrealistic rules for how we and others 'should' behave: 'I should have been given more time for this.'

You may assume you are actually motivating yourself with 'should' and 'ought to.' For example, 'I should have been able to do this really well and got it finished on time.' In fact, as with all the other examples of negative self-talk, thoughts like this simply create more anxiety.

Perfectionist thinking

The negative self-talk of a perfectionist tells you that you and the things you do are not good enough. Again, the words 'should', 'must', 'ought to', etc. are used a lot. This creates anxiety by pushing you to your physical and mental limits, which results in ongoing stress.

Personalization

Personalization is a cognitive distortion where you believe that everything is about you; that what others do or say is some kind of direct, personal reaction to you. You might also believe that if events don't turn out well, then it's your fault. You may also compare yourself to others trying to determine who is smarter, better looking, etc. 'What if I've got nothing in common with them? What if they think I'm boring? I just know I've only been invited because my friends want me to make up numbers.'

Emotional reasoning

With emotional reasoning, you believe that you are what you feel. If, for example, you *feel* stupid and boring, then you assume you must *be* stupid and boring.

Victimization

This self-talk is characterized by moaning, complaining and blaming. If events don't go well, you feel deceived or let down or burdened, either by your own emotions or lack of knowledge or by other people: 'It's not fair. What have we done to deserve this?' and 'I should have been given more time for this. I'll be in trouble with my manager. She'll use this against me.'

Negative thinking and anxiety work together to create a spiral of unhelpful thoughts and difficult feelings; this means that when you're anxious you interpret things negatively. And when you interpret things negatively, you feed your anxiety.

Negative self-talk also tells you that you have little or no control over your circumstances.

Learned helplessness

As we go about our daily lives, each of us is continually thinking, interpreting and assessing our circumstances, experiences, events and situations.

To make sense of the events and experiences, we each have an 'explanatory style'. What this means is that when something happens, has happened or is going to happen, our brains automatically look for an explanation that makes sense to us – one that fits our usual way of interpreting events. If you have developed a habit of negative thinking, you will continue to return to this way of thinking, interpreting and explaining events. And each time you do, your brain uses those same neural pathways and you strengthen that habit of thinking, interpreting and explaining things.

These negative ways of thinking can lead to a phenomenon called 'learned helplessness.' What this means is that because your negative thinking and cognitive distortions have convinced you of the hopelessness of a situation, you have, in effect, 'learnt' – or rather, you've 'taught' yourself – that you have little or no control over the outcome of a situation.

You end up with a kind of tunnel vision that means you only see evidence of what you already think and believe. In other words, having 'learned' to believe in your limitations and lack of control, you unwittingly gather evidence that reinforces those limitations and lack of control.

Even when you are made aware of your negative thinking and even if there's evidence that things won't turn out badly and you could see things more positively, it can be a real struggle to convince yourself of a more logical and reasoned response. Your explanatory style is to see things negatively.

The good news, though, is that your way of interpreting events is not permanent and your outlook is not fixed. You can overcome negative thinking by learning new explanatory styles; you *can* learn to think in a more positive, helpful way.

Becoming more aware of your thoughts

The first step in managing negative self-talk is simply to be aware of it. A simple way to do this is to write it down in a 'Thought Diary'. Don't let the sound of this put you off – it doesn't need to be hard or time-consuming. Just get a pen and paper and keep it to hand. Or text or email your thoughts to yourself.

As you go about your day, if you are feeling uneasy or less than calm and relaxed, you may have negative thoughts streaming through your head that you weren't aware of. So, whenever you are feeling anxious or upset, use this as your signal to stop and become aware of your thoughts. Use your feelings as your cue to reflect on how you are thinking.

You won't be aware of every single thought, but when you do notice a negative or unpleasant thought, write it down. It doesn't need to be word for word in great detail – a quick note will do.

When you do notice a negative thought, don't pass any judgement on yourself for having this thought. Just be aware of it and write it down. After a few days you may notice a bit of a pattern or theme emerging. You may notice, for example, what sort of events and experiences trigger your negative thoughts.

Kate kept a Thought Diary for a week:

> 'I wrote about events as they happened and the thoughts
> I attached to situations and events. For example, when I

missed the bus I found myself thinking, "Why does this always happen to me?"

I also wrote about upcoming events. I wrote down my self-talk about telling my parents I didn't want them to visit this weekend as I wanted to spend the weekend with my boys. I wrote down my thoughts about meeting a friend for lunch and I also wrote down my thoughts and self-talk about a doctor's appointment I had at the end of the week.

I was surprised at just how often I attached negative thoughts to all these events. Even when a friend said she'd come with me to the doctors, instead of keeping focused on the fact that she would be coming with me, I moved on to worrying about what the doctor would think of me. I started thinking, "I just know the doctor is going to think I'm being ridiculous having a friend come with me about an ingrowing toenail."

Keeping a track of my thoughts helped me identify patterns in my thinking, to understand how I see myself, other people, situations and events. I realize that so often I jump to conclusions, catastrophize and think I "know" what other people will be thinking.'

Nick also kept a Thought Diary. He realized the negative things he said most often to himself were usually along the same lines. He called them his 'negative stories'. They included the 'my friends are better than me' story and the 'I don't get things done well enough' story. He discovered he had much the same 'stories' most of the time, which helped him to realize the fact that they had become habits – habitual ways of thinking, not necessarily truthful ways of thinking.

Like Nick and Kate, if you keep a diary of events and associated thoughts and feelings, you can begin to identify your own 'explanatory style'.

You may not consciously be aware of your self-talk – your subconscious mind is taking it all in. It simply accepts everything you tell it and responds accordingly. Physical and behavioural reactions are triggered, which prompts more negative self-talk, and a self-perpetuating downward spiral begins. But once you are more aware of your negative self-talk, you can start to do something about it.

In a nutshell

- Negative thoughts can be self-perpetuating, leaving no room for more positive, helpful ways of thinking.
- Regardless of whether your thoughts and actions are positive or negative, they become a habit, which means that any negative thinking patterns can become your normal way of thinking.
- As we grew up, we may have been discouraged from questioning and contradicting what we were told. This can mean that we suppress the instinct to question how logical, realistic or helpful our own thoughts are.
- Your self-talk has a way of creating its own reality. Telling yourself you can do something can help it happen. Telling yourself you *can't* do something can make that more likely to be true.
- Thinking in negative, unhelpful ways is also known as 'cognitive distortion.' There's a range of ways in which cognitive distortions occur: jumping to a conclusion,

catastrophizing, overgeneralization, mind reading and tunnel thinking.

- Cognitive distortions are powerful because they can easily convince you that your thoughts are rational and true. But actually, they are limiting, unhelpful and even destructive.
- To make sense of events and experiences, we each have an 'explanatory style' – our own way of thinking, interpreting and explaining events.
- The first step in managing negative self-talk is simply to be aware of it by writing it down. Once you are more aware of your negative self-talk, you can start to do something about it.

PART TWO

Managing Anxiety

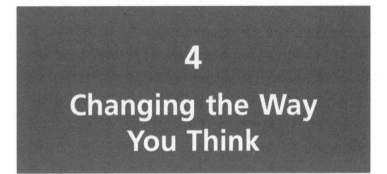

4

Changing the Way You Think

Self-talk happens. We all do it. So, if you're going to have constant thoughts going through your head, you may as well make most of them positive rather than negative. The next step, then, is to change your way of thinking, to get out of a negative thinking rut.

But just how do you replace unhelpful, irrational and disempowering beliefs with more realistic, useful and empowering ones? If negative self-talk came with an off switch, you could just flip it. But it doesn't. It takes some effective techniques, effort and practice in order to dispute negative thoughts and replace them with more helpful ones. But you can do it and it is worth the effort!

Challenging your self-talk

Challenging your self-talk means challenging the negative or unhelpful aspects: the cognitive distortions such as generalizing, mind reading and tunnel thinking. Doing this enables you to see whether your view is reasonable and, if not, identify more helpful ways of thinking instead. You can then move on to responding to situations in a more constructive, helpful way.

There are three main types of challenging questions you can ask yourself:

1. Questions about the reality of your thinking: how much of what you think could happen is real and true rather than imaginary?
2. Questions about perspective: how does what you think and believe relate to and measure against other possibilities, taking everything else into account?
3. Questions about alternative explanations: other ways of interpreting and explaining things.

1. Questions about reality
- What is the evidence for what I think will happen?
- What is the evidence against what I think?
- In what way is it helpful for me to think like this?

2. Questions about perspective
- What is the worst thing that could happen? How likely is it?
- What is the best thing that could happen?
- What is most likely to happen?
- Is there anything good about this situation?

3. Questions about alternative explanations
- How would a more positive friend perceive this? What would they say to me?

- If the situation was reversed, what positive things would I say to a friend if they were the one thinking negatively about this?

Let's take the example of Jess from the previous chapter. Jess was concerned about driving down from Doncaster to London to start a new job. She had never done this journey by car before. Last time she drove somewhere new she got lost. Jess was feeling anxious and panicky about it: 'I'll never get there. I won't be able to sleep the night before so then I'll be too tired to think straight. I just know I'll be stressed and I'll get horribly lost.'

Questions about reality
- Evidence for and against what I think will happen.
    - Evidence for: I got horribly lost when I drove to Bristol last month.
    - Against: I have driven to other new places before and I didn't always get lost.
- In what way is it helpful for me to think like this? It isn't!

Questions about perspective
- What is the worst thing that could happen? How likely is it?
    I will get lost. I will be stressed.
- What is the best thing that could happen?
    I get there without getting het up. I arrive feeling calm.
- What is most likely to happen?
    I'll get lost!
- Is there anything good about this situation?
    I got the job! I start next week.

Questions about alternative explanations

- How would a more positive friend perceive this? What would they say to me?

    'Is there anything I can do to help? Shall I come over and we could talk through the best way to do this?'

- If the situation were reversed, what positive things would I say to a friend in this situation?

    'You don't have to do it all in one go. You could drive to your sister's in Leicester first. You could buy a satnav. You *can* do it!'

Remember, when you feel anxious and stressed, your self-talk is likely to dismiss or ignore the helpful possibilities and options. You'll more likely expect the worst and focus on the most negative aspects of your situation. Recognizing that your current way of thinking might be self-defeating can prompt you to look at things from a different perspective.

This doesn't mean that you ignore or pretend you don't have those anxious thoughts. Rather, you identify and acknowledge the negative thinking.

Questioning your thoughts is a useful step towards interrupting your habit of negative self-talk.

Replacing negative self-talk and cognitive distortions with positive self-talk

When you're anxious it's not easy to say positive things to yourself. But you can replace negative thoughts with positive thoughts.

Think of a time when something didn't turn out as you would have liked: a job, a project, a holiday, a relationship or a friendship. What were your thoughts? Write them down. If they were negative, what other, more positive thoughts might have been possible instead?

If you are struggling with this, a useful way to do it is to think of yourself as a script writer – imagine you are simply writing alternative thoughts for a character in a play.

Now look at the thoughts you've written down in a 'Thought Diary'. Look at each one and come up with some ideas for more positive thoughts to replace the negative self-talk.

Avoid going to the opposite extreme though – keep it possible and believable for you. For example, if one of your regular thoughts has been, 'I'm such an idiot! I'm always making mistakes, everyone must think I'm stupid', it doesn't need to become, 'I'm brilliant! I do everything really well. People are in awe of me.' That's just another cognitive distortion – an overly positive one! Instead, replace it with something like, 'I always try to do my best. Sometimes I make mistakes. We all do. I can start again.'

Do make the new positive thought something that *feels* believable to you, otherwise your mind will not accept it as a real possibility.

It's important to know that neither negative thinking nor positive thinking is more 'real' or 'true' than the other. Either way of thinking could be real or true. But what does make one way of thinking more real is the one you choose to say to yourself. As Shakespeare said, 'For there is nothing either good or bad, but thinking makes it so.'

Take control of your brain

Anything and everything, then, can be explained in a positive or negative way. The trick is to choose the most positive explanation and to tell that to yourself. (Now and again, when it's appropriate, try saying it out loud.) Then consider realistic reasons why the positive explanation could be logical, rational, real and true.

Supposing, for example, you were an impatient type of person. The negative way to view impatience is to see it as an inability to wait or accept delay: to push for things to happen too quickly. But it's also true that if you are impatient then you move things forward and you *do* make things happen and get things done. Which is the true definition? Whichever one you choose to believe.

Remember, '*Nothing* is either good or bad, but *thinking* makes it so.'

You can take this further by looking up words like 'impatience' in the dictionary. Try looking up the words 'opportunistic', 'opinionated', 'slow' and 'curious'. You'll see that the definitions are pretty neutral. It's only the way that you interpret those words that makes the definition negative or positive.

By changing the way you think, you can positively influence how you respond to situations. This is the premise behind Cognitive Behavioural Therapy (CBT).

CBT is based on the idea that the way we think about situations can affect the way we feel and behave; if you interpret a situation in a certain way, you will respond accordingly.

With CBT you identify and challenge any negative thinking patterns and behaviour which may be causing you difficulties. This can then change the way you feel about situations and enable you to change your behaviour in future.

Making positive self-talk a habit

It's helpful if you can write down your more positive thoughts, especially when you first start replacing negative thoughts with positive ones. Writing the positive thoughts down helps to anchor the ideas in your mind.

'I use an app for this: "Thought Diary Pro". I can tap in the situation, my thoughts, how helpful that thought is, what a more helpful thought might be and so on. It's on my phone and I have it with me always. I feel less conspicuous using it than if I was getting out a pen and paper.'

You could even make a list of helpful, positive responses for the things you know you most often say to yourself. You could write your positive responses on little 'coping cards', or text them to yourself so you can look at them when you need to.

For example, if you often say, 'I'm so slow, I must be thick and stupid', your positive response might be, 'I'm not slow, thick or stupid. *I just need time to process things so I understand them properly*', where your focus is on the words that are in italic.

You have to choose which way to think. It's a choice. Only you can make that choice. No one can force you to think more positively.

When you do become aware of a negative thought, acknowledge it but don't get angry or annoyed with yourself for thinking in this way. Instead, think of a more positive response – a more helpful way of looking at things – and focus your attention on that. Focus your thoughts on things that are good and positive. Allow yourself to imagine the best that could happen.

Frame your thoughts in positive words and language

Small, simple tweaks in the words you use can make a big difference to your self-talk.

For example, thinking, 'I am not going to lie awake all night worrying about this!' uses three negative terms: 'not', 'worry' and 'lie awake'. Instead, say something like, 'I am going to bed to rest and I will sleep when it comes.'

And, instead of saying, 'I *won't* get there for another hour,' a more positive way of saying this would be to simply say, 'I will get there in an hour.'

Instead of, 'I won't know until tomorrow', leave out the words 'won't' and 'until' and instead, simply say, 'I will know tomorrow'.

Here are some more ideas about the words and language you use that can help you to be more positive.

'And' not 'but'

Look at these two sentences:

'I went to the shop but I forgot to buy the milk.'

'I wrote the report but there was one item I didn't include.'

'But' is a minimizing word that detracts from the thought or statement before it. By using the word 'but', you've minimized the fact that you went to the shop and still managed to buy the other things you needed. In the case of the report, you've minimized that you have, in fact, written it.

A small, effective trick is to replace the word 'but' by 'and'. It can create a much more positive meaning.

Read out loud the two sentences and notice how different it feels to say them this time.

'I went to the shops *and* I forgot to buy the milk.'

'I wrote the report *and* there was one item I didn't include.'

(*Continued*)

By using the word 'and', you make it more likely that you will also come up with a solution. 'But' is final; 'and' infers there's still more to come, as you can read here:

> 'I went to the shops and I forgot to buy the milk. *I'll buy some after lunch.*'

> 'I wrote the report and there was one item I didn't include. *I'll add it tomorrow.*'

Should or could?

Instead of saying 'should' or 'shouldn't', try using 'could', 'will' or 'going to' instead. Using the word 'could' instead of 'should' suggests that you do, in fact, have a choice as to whether you do something or not. This shift in use of words is a kinder and more flexible approach. Rather than suggesting that someone or something is expecting or making you do something – which adds pressure that creates more anxiety – you are making a choice about what to think and do or not think and do.

To give a similar example, instead of saying you 'can't' do something, say you 'aren't going' to do it. 'Can't' suggests you want to but someone or something is stopping you. 'Aren't' or 'won't' is a clear declaration that you are choosing and taking responsibility for doing it or not doing it.

Never ever and always

Words like 'always' and 'never' are frequently misused and inappropriate because the statements that include them are rarely true. For instance, 'I always forget things' is probably not true. You don't *always* forget things really, do you? It would be far more realistic to say 'I sometimes forget things.'

Be more conscious – and conscientious – about the words you use.

It's perfectly okay to pause and organize your thoughts so that you can phrase your self-talk – and what you say out loud – in a positive way. And if you catch yourself using negative words and phrases midsentence, stop and re-phrase what you want to say in more positive terms.

With practice, you can learn to notice your own negative self-talk as it happens, and consciously choose to think about the situation in a more helpful way. You can also learn a lot about the effect of the language we all use just by listening to other people. Listen to the people around you and to people talking on the TV and radio. Listen out for negative words and phrases and try and think of positive alternatives.

Remember, your self-talk *can* be positive, kind, encouraging and empowering. You can change some of the negative aspects of your thinking by challenging the unhelpful parts and replacing them with more reasonable words and thoughts.

Changing the way you think

Learning how to change the way you think and behave is a really effective step towards managing anxiety. You may be wondering, though, how long it takes to change a habit of negative thinking into a habit of positive thinking. Ten days? Three weeks? A couple of months? It's different for everyone; there are no hard and fast rules.

Change – in the way you think or what you do – requires you to let go of the old, established ways of doing things and be open to new ideas and approaches. And that takes some time because changing from one way of doing things to another, and thinking or doing things differently is part of a process – a series of steps you need to take in order to do things differently.

It's helpful to understand this process of change and how it relates to overcoming anxiety. There are four stages:

1. At first, you are unaware of the possibility or need to change the way you think. You worry and get anxious. It's what you do. You probably avoid any discussion about it being a problem.
2. At some point, though, you move on to the next stage, where you recognize and accept that worrying and being anxious is a problem for you. You want things to change and you're open to possible solutions, ideas and advice. Reading this book, for example, means that you're at this stage.

    You know that it's not going to be easy to change the way you think but you also recognize the benefits of changing and intend to take steps to help you do something about it.
3. The next stage is the action stage – the stage when you actually make the changes to what you do and/ or think. You try out new ways of thinking and behaving and you try to maintain those changes.

4. Finally, a new habit is established – it becomes the new normal way of thinking or doing.

Is it that straightforward? No. This process of changing the way you think doesn't necessarily follow a simple linear progression. It's more of a cycle of change and you are likely to move through the cycle a number of times before fully establishing more positive ways of thinking.

The good news is that you don't necessarily fall back to where you started. Usually, you make progress and then slip back a few times until the new ways become your new normal way of thinking and behaving.

It's important that you remember this, so that if you do slip back to your old ways of thinking and behaving, you don't lose hope and give up but are motivated to get back into thinking and behaving more positively.

Just know that every time you do think positively, you're more likely to think that way again. Remember the science: because of the interconnections between the nerve cells in your brain, when you think or do something new, you create new connections – neural pathways – in your brain. If your brain continues using these new pathways, they become stronger and deeper. Eventually, they will replace the old ways of thinking and behaving.

Train your brain to accept change
You can help the process of changing the way you think by training your brain to adapt to change. Try this:

> Move the clock or the wastepaper bin to a different place in your room at home or at work.
>
> See how long it takes you to stop looking in the wrong place for the time or throwing rubbish on the floor. Yes, it is disorientating but choosing to break a routine way of doing things on a regular basis can be a powerful tactic in getting used to changing the way you think.

Make a conscious effort to be flexible and adapt to change. You only need to make small changes. For example, take a different route from the one you'd usually take around the supermarket. Walk a new route to work or drive a different route from the one you would usually take when you visit friends and family. Listen to a different radio station from the one you normally listen to.

Studies have shown that people will keep the same familiar ways of thinking and doing things – like what they eat for breakfast, how they get dressed, where they park their car and so on – every time if they're in the same environment. But if they go on holiday, it's more likely that the behaviour will change. That's one of the reasons why taking a holiday or short break away can be good for you: it can help break certain habits.

Whether you are at home, at work or on holiday, if you do things differently you'll experience different results. What new things could you do? Start today; get used to being flexible and able to change. This will help you to think differently – to change your self-talk.

Train your brain to be more positive

As well as training your brain to think differently, there are ways you can train your brain to be more positive. And the more you train your brain to think positively, the more likely you'll have helpful, positive thoughts and beliefs that will help you to manage and overcome anxiety.

Noticing the good things

Noticing what's good really encourages positive thinking, because when you think about the positive events and people in your life, you access and strengthen those positive neural pathways.

Here is a simple but very effective technique for developing positivity:

> Before you go to bed each night, identify three good things that have happened during the day. You could write them down, but you may simply reflect on what those things are while you are brushing your teeth.
>
> They only need to be small, simple things. For example: it rained and you'd remembered your umbrella; a friend sent a nice text; you watched something good on TV; you enjoyed something new to eat; someone told you something interesting or made you laugh; you heard a favourite song on the radio.

'Writing about good things that happened that day helps me to put aside the nonsense that my mind creates. It doesn't matter how small the event is, so long as it's something.'

Whether you've had a good day or not, identify and reflect on the small pleasures that happened. I really recommend you try and make this a habit. Just make an effort every day for a couple of weeks to identify the good things in your day and then think about them for a few minutes. You will soon find yourself actively looking for things to appreciate and, after a while, it will become second nature.

Research shows that people who do this even sleep better, probably because they think fewer negative thoughts – and more positive ones – just before going to sleep.

Positive passwords

When you're choosing passwords for Internet accounts, choose positive words and phrases such as 'kindness' (make it a strong password by using non-alphabetical characters too – 'k!ndne88', for example) or 'enjoyment'. Or use words that remind you of good times – people, places or things that evoke positive thoughts. Recalling positive words will prompt your brain to access positive neural pathways.

Be kind

> 'Happiness, I realize, is looking up and out and at other things. It is taking a keen interest in the world around you and not the one in your head.'
>
> Bryony Gordon

Helping other people and doing kind acts gets you into a cycle of positive thinking because it requires you to actively look for – to be aware of and notice – positive ways to connect with other people. Kind gestures free you from focusing on yourself and enable you to reach out to someone else.

Who in your life could benefit from an act of kindness and compassion – someone who is lonely, unwell or worried and anxious themselves, perhaps? You may feel you have little to offer, but whether it is a smile, a cup of tea, an invite to dinner or an offer to help carry or collect something, it is the act of giving itself that is important.

Get in touch with someone you haven't talked to in a while. Phone or write them a card, email or text to let them know you were thinking about them.

Treat someone to cake. It could be your colleagues, neighbours, family or friends; whoever you choose, surprise them by bringing in a homemade or shop-bought cake. In the summer, bring in some fresh fruit – strawberries or melon.

Another way to make a positive connection is the next time you read something on someone's blog or website that inspires you or makes you smile, let them know. Write a positive review or comment. You can also make a point of noticing the good work someone has done. It could be someone who serves you in a shop or café. Make a positive comment about their work or business.

Finally, notice what someone is wearing and how they look. Compliments (appropriate compliments) on appearance make people feel good.

Positive visualization

It's not just what you say to yourself; what you see can also help you to think in a more positive, optimistic way. The more you imagine yourself coping and coming out the other side, the more likely it is to happen.

Think of a time when you coped with – and successfully came through – a difficult or challenging situation. Picture what happened, where you were, what you did, what other people said and did.

Remind yourself of these times as a way of helping yourself to have positive thoughts and images.

When you're replacing negative thoughts with more positive ones, create new images for yourself. Visualize new possibilities – pictures where you are coping and managing and things turn out well.

Jess did this: 'I bought a satnav and learnt how to use it on familiar journeys. A few days before I drove to London, I visualized driving to London and saw myself calmly following the instructions on the satnav. Instead of playing out the worst scenario in my mind, I visualized the best outcome.'

Visualization is important, because seeing yourself coping makes your brain believe that it *is*, indeed, possible. The future you see is the future you get. In Chapter 7 we look at ways to turn visualization into action.

In a nutshell

- Your self-talk can be positive, kind, encouraging and empowering.
- You don't need to try and ignore your negative thoughts or pretend you don't have anxious thoughts. Rather, you identify and acknowledge the negative

thinking and aim to replace it with more reasonable, helpful thoughts.

- Neither negative nor positive ways of thinking are more 'real' or 'true' than the other. But what does make one way of thinking more real and true is simply the one you choose to say to yourself.

- Your positive thoughts need to *feel believable to you, otherwise your mind will not accept them as real possibilities.*

- Be more conscious – and conscientious – about the words you use; frame your thoughts in positive words and language.

- Change requires you to let go of the old, established ways of doing things and be open to new ideas and approaches.

- You can help the process of changing the way you think by training your brain to adapt to change.

- If you do slip back to your old ways of thinking and behaving, keep the faith. Every time you do think positively, you're more likely to think that way again.

- There are ways you can train your brain to be more positive: notice the good things in your day, for example, or look for ways to connect with and help others.

- The more you train your brain to think positively, the more likely you'll have helpful, positive thoughts and beliefs that will help you to manage and overcome anxiety.

- Visualize new possibilities – pictures where you are coping and managing and things turn out well. Instead of playing out the worst scenario in your mind, visualize the best outcome.

- Seeing yourself coping makes your brain believe that it is, indeed, possible.

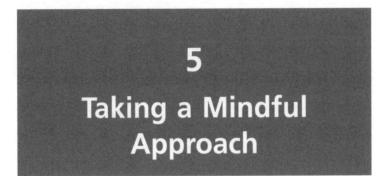

5
Taking a Mindful Approach

Learning how to be mindful can be a great help in managing and overcoming anxiety. There are two forms of mindfulness – formal mindfulness and informal mindfulness.

Formal mindfulness involves meditation. For many people, meditation, meditation classes and guided meditation CDs and apps can be very helpful with managing anxiety.

In this chapter we will be looking at informal mindfulness. This means taking a mindful *approach*.

Mindfulness is about being in the present moment. Worry and anxiety, though, take you out of the present moment and into the future – an unknown future – where doubts, fears and negative thoughts dominate your mind. Imagine, for example, you've been asked to organize a friend's birthday party. It's nothing too big – just a meal for a few friends one evening next week. The pressure is on; you're feeling stressed and worry if you've chosen the right restaurant, if everyone will come and if they'll enjoy it.

By taking a mindful approach, instead of worrying and pre-living the future, you acknowledge potential difficulties, but then you focus on what you *can* manage and control, now in the present moment.

Because staying in the present is an essential part of overcoming anxiety, a mindful approach can help you to steer your focus away from future possibilities. This can help you to feel calmer, more in control and able to manage.

There are several aspects and qualities to mindfulness. They are:

Awareness and acknowledgement: Being aware of thoughts, experiences and events that are happening in the present moment.

Acceptance: Knowing that thoughts, feelings, sensations and beliefs are just that – thoughts, feelings, sensations and beliefs. You don't have to react to them.

Non-judgement: Not judging your thoughts, feelings and experiences. Instead, you simply experience or observe them; you know you don't need to give any meaning to your thoughts and feelings, other people's actions and events, etc.

Letting go: Not getting attached to or stuck in your thoughts, feelings and beliefs, people, things and events.

Beginner's mind: With beginner's mind, rather than respond to feelings, experiences and events in the ways you usually do (ways from the past), you open yourself up to new possibilities – to doing things in new ways.

Focus and engagement: Managing your attention so that it is focused only on what's happening now. You are concentrating on and involved with only what's happening right now.

Patience: Understanding that things develop and move forward in their own time.

All these aspects and qualities of mindfulness can work together to help you manage worries and anxiety.

Firstly, the mindful qualities of awareness, acknowledgement, acceptance, being non-judgemental and letting go can help you to be aware of when you're getting caught up in anxious thoughts and feelings. These mindful qualities can also help you to know that thoughts are simply 'mental events' that do not have to have control over you; you can accept and acknowledge them and then let them go.

Secondly, the mindful qualities of beginner's mind, patience, focus and engagement can help you to gain a sense of perspective, think positively and feel more capable of managing situations and events.

'Taking a mindful approach helped me to realize when I've got myself trapped "pre-living" future events or possibilities.'

Awareness, acceptance, acknowledgement, non-judgement and letting go

Being aware, acknowledging, accepting and being non-judgemental

Analysing what, how and why you feel like you do can just make you feel more het up and anxious.

Mindful acceptance and acknowledgement encourage you to understand that, for whatever reason and however illogical, 'wrong' or 'ridiculous' it might seem, you do feel like you do. Rather than analyse, judge, fight or suppress worrying and anxious thoughts, you first just acknowledge that they're there. Then you accept them and allow your thoughts to come and go.

Being prepared to experience anxiety will lead to less anxiety overall. If you can learn to experience difficult, anxious thoughts and feelings until they naturally pass – and they will pass – you won't need to use avoidance coping.

For example, you might say to yourself, 'Here's the thought that I might fail my exam/I won't get the job/I won't know anyone at the party.' Or, instead of telling yourself, 'I'm so disorganized, I'll never get anything done,' you might say, 'I'm having a thought that I'm not going to get it done.'

It can help if you think of yourself as an observer – as just *watching* your thoughts. There's no need to judge your thinking as 'wrong', 'ridiculous' or 'stupid'. A negative, anxious thought is just a negative, anxious thought. It is what it is.

One way to think of yourself as an observer with no opinions about your thoughts is with this simple exercise: Choose a colour – red, for example – and for the next minute, notice everything around you that's the colour red. It's relatively easy to do this – to just notice, and accept without trying to change anything. This is what you're aiming for when you notice and observe your anxious thoughts.

Let go

Once you've acknowledged and accepted anxious thoughts, the next step is to let them go. Here are some ways that you can imagine letting go of worries, fears and concerns:

- As people passing you by as you sit on a park bench or in a café;
- As items on a conveyer belt;
- As train carriages passing on a track;
- As clouds floating past in the sky;
- As helium balloons floating up into the sky.

Each time a worrying thought enters your mind, you acknowledge it and let it go. There is no need to try to change the thought, or argue with it or judge it; just be aware, acknowledge, accept and let it pass. Just see each thought as simply a mental event and visualize it passing by. Calmly tell yourself an affirmative phrase such as, 'This, too, shall pass.'

This takes practice. It means thinking differently about your thoughts – that is, you *don't* think about your thoughts!

Write it down

Instead of letting thoughts swirl around your mind, another way to acknowledge, accept and let go of anxious thoughts and feelings is to externalize them by writing them down.

Writing down thoughts, fears and worries is a good way to empty your mind. You're then free to focus on the present: on what's happening or what you can do right now.

Either write down the anxious thought on paper (keep a pen and paper handy) or make use of an app such as Thought Diary Pro mentioned in Chapter 4. Then, you can literally observe the worry, concern or anxious thought and let it go by closing the notepad, laptop or phone.

If, after that, the worries, fears, anxious thoughts, etc. pop up again, say to yourself, 'Stop! I already worried' and 'I can worry about that later.' Then divert your thoughts to another activity. (You may need to make a list of these possible diversions beforehand. The part about 'flow' in Chapter 7 can help you with this.)

You might find it helpful to go back over what you wrote a few weeks later and see what happened. Events you were worrying about either didn't happen, or one way or another were managed. And if things did not turn out well, you can look at what you learnt from that experience that could inform the next one – more about this in Chapter 7.

Tell someone
It can be hard to share private thoughts and concerns, but another of the ways you could acknowledge and let go of anxious thoughts is to tell someone else what you're worried about – what negative, anxious thoughts are going through your mind. You might just want them to listen or you might want their advice and support. Chapter 9 discusses how other people can help you.

'I have spent a long time suffering from anxiety. I'm only just starting to feel I can accept this and be open about it without feeling like I have, in some way, done something wrong or that I've failed or that there's something wrong with me.'

Beginner's mind, focus, engagement and patience

Once you have acknowledged, accepted and let worries and anxious thoughts pass, the mindful qualities of beginner's mind, patience, focus and engagement can help you to think positively, gain a sense of perspective and feel more capable of managing and overcoming the anxiety.

Beginner's mind

Worry and anxiety can often be triggered by the memory of a past event and experience that didn't go well. Then, when you have a similar situation coming up, you can find yourself reliving that past experience, which then triggers doubts, fears and anxiety about that forthcoming situation or event.

Joe, for example, was tying himself up in knots worrying about telling his parents that they couldn't come to visit and stay with him next weekend. (He had too many other things going on at the time.)

Last time he tried to put his parents off, they were offended and things got difficult between them. Joe is sure they'll respond in the same way this time. He's feeling stressed and anxious about telling them.

You may remember reading in Chapter 3 that Jess was worried about driving to London on her own, having got lost the last time she drove somewhere new.

If you're like Joe and Jess, it only takes one event to turn out badly to 'prove' that things can go wrong, and that you are 'right' to worry. But a reaction based on the past doesn't allow you to be aware of any new insights and of new ways to think and do things.

'Beginner's mind', on the other hand, encourages you to put aside what you 'know' will happen as a result of past experience. Instead, you think about what you *learned* from that past situation that you can use to make the next experience a better one. Ask yourself, 'How can I begin again – make this experience different and more positive than the last time?'

Joe, for example, decided that what he could do that was different was to suggest some different dates for his parents to visit. Dates that Joe could commit to when he didn't have so much going on and would feel less stressed. Jess's new approach was to buy a satnav and practise using it.

Thinking of new possibilities can reduce worry and anxiety because you focus your thinking on what you can do differently. You replace negative thinking with positive thinking.

So, if you're worried about repeating the same experience again, one that was difficult, distressing or painful, think about something new that you can do this time around. Know that you *can* make it different from last time. We'll look at positive action you can take in Chapter 7.

Focus and engagement

Often, when you're worried and anxious, your mind is flitting between a number of negative, unhelpful and distressing thoughts. Mindfulness encourages you to focus on the present and engage your mind with more helpful thoughts.

For Joe and Jess, this meant focusing their minds on problem solving, on being 'solution-focused.' What this meant was that rather than let their minds be filled with anxious thoughts, they focused on how they could positively manage their situations.

Another way to use mindful focus and engagement is as a distraction technique. For example, if you were anxious about an interview the next day and you had done all you could to prepare for it, you might focus and engage your mind with something else the evening before: a good film or a meal out with friends. There is more about how you can use mindful focus and engagement in Chapter 7.

Patience

Negative self-talk and cognitive distortions make it easy to jump to conclusions about things that will either happen in their own time or won't even actually happen. Mindfulness encourages you to be patient; to know that whatever you're worried about, when that time comes, you can act on it then.

Mindful patience can slow down those thoughts that are racing in front of you; it can help you to experience anxious thoughts and feelings until they naturally pass. In fact, you might say to yourself, 'This, too, shall pass.'

You can encourage patience with mindful breathing techniques (see the next chapter) and calm, reassuring self-talk. This means saying the sort of things you would say to a friend if you were helping them to stop jumping ahead of themselves. Saying things like, 'It's going to be OK. You *can* deal with things as they happen.'

It's important to know that these aspects and qualities of mindfulness – acceptance, awareness, beginner's mind, etc. – are dynamic. That is, although they have distinctive characteristics, each aspect is linked to and interacts with other aspects. So, for example, if you approach a situation with '*beginner's mind*', you are likely to be able to *let go* of thoughts, ideas, ways of doing things, etc. from the past. This then means that you can *accept* that past events are just that – in the past.

If, on the other hand, you start by approaching a situation with *acceptance* and *patience*, you are more likely to be able to *let go* of troubling thoughts, doubts and worries. This will then mean you are able to tackle what's worrying you with a fresh approach – with a *beginner's mind*.

Acceptance and Commitment Therapy

Acceptance and Commitment Therapy (ACT) is one of the recent mindfulness-based behaviour therapies and coaching models that can be effective in managing anxiety.

Acceptance and Commitment Therapy works in much the same way as I've described a mindful approach to managing anxiety in the previous pages. It involves learning to accept what may be out of your personal control, while committing to action that will improve your quality of life, both in the short term and the long term.

Instead of spending energy struggling, avoiding or obsessing over anxious thoughts, you acknowledge them, learn not to react or avoid situations that trigger them. You also learn to clarify what is important and meaningful to you – your values – then use that knowledge to motivate and guide you to improve your situation and circumstances.

Typically, when you're anxious you become caught up in your thoughts. ACT calls this being 'fused' with your thoughts. You judge your thinking and you judge yourself for the thoughts you have. Not only are you anxious but you're angry and/or upset with your anxiety: 'Not again. Why do I always feel like this?' 'What's wrong with me? 'Why do I feel so awful?' It's a vicious circle.

You may try to avoid whatever it is that makes you anxious (limiting your life and your experiences) or respond in inappropriate ways and try to justify or make excuses for why you think or behave as you do.

Anxiety can be seen as like falling into a pool of quicksand. The more a person struggles, the faster it sucks them under; struggling is the worst thing you can possibly do. ACT suggests that the way to survive is to lie back, spread out your arms and float on the surface. It's not easy because every instinct tells you to struggle, but if you do so, you'll go under. The same principle applies to difficult feelings: the more you try to fight them, the more they overwhelm you.

ACT suggests that you don't struggle. So, if anxiety shows up then, yes, it's unpleasant and very uncomfortable. You don't like it or want it, but importantly, you don't spend time and energy struggling with it.

ACT breaks mindfulness skills down into three areas:

- *Awareness and acceptance:* Making room for painful feelings, urges and sensations, and allowing them to come and go without a struggle.
- *Observing the self and 'defusion':* Distancing yourself from, and letting go of, unhelpful thoughts, beliefs and memories.
- *Identifying your values and committing to action:* Working out what's important to you and doing something helpful, based on what's important.

Awareness and acceptance

With awareness and acceptance, you notice your anxious thoughts and feelings and learn to let them come and go without struggling with them or fixating on them.

Start by being aware of your unease. Step back for a moment and comment on how you feel. Keep it simple. Say to yourself, 'I'm starting to work myself up and I'm scaring myself.' Or 'I can feel myself getting more and more nervous right now.' Or 'I'm sitting here thinking how bad this could get.'

Next, allow those anxious thoughts and feelings to be there – accept them without trying to change them.

One way to do this that I've already described is to say to yourself, 'Here's the thought that I might fail my exam/I won't get the job/I won't know anyone at the party.' Another way is to be aware of everything that's one colour – red, for example.

A popular and simple mindfulness exercise that can also help you here is focused on eating chocolate. Take a piece of chocolate (or any sweet that melts) and let it slowly melt in your mouth. Focus on the taste and texture, sounds, sensations and movements inside your mouth.

While you're doing this, other distracting thoughts and feelings may arise. The aim is simply to accept those thoughts, allow them to come and go, all the while keeping your attention focused on eating the chocolate.

So, whenever you're anxious you could chew gum or suck a sweet and focus on that. At the same time, allow anxious feelings to arise and pass. (Try not to eat too many sweets though – make this a short-term approach!)

If, for example, you are someone who experiences social anxiety, you might be so caught up in struggling with anxious thoughts and feelings that you are unable to take part in even the simplest of conversations. The analogy with the mindful chocolate and sweets eating is that, just as you focused on the chocolate, in social situations, focus on the other person or people rather than on your anxious thoughts and feelings.

Observing the self and cognitive defusion
There are two parts to your mind. Your thinking mind is responsible for all your thoughts, beliefs, memories, judgements, etc. Then there's your observing mind – the part of your mind that is able to notice what you are thinking.

For example, you might think, 'I wonder how Jane is. I hope she's OK now.' Your observing mind might then think, 'Golly, I haven't thought about Jane for a long time.' So, there are your thoughts, and there is you noticing them.

Cognitive defusion involves stepping back and detaching from anxious thoughts and worries; instead of getting caught up or fused with your thoughts, or struggling to get rid of them, you learn to notice them and to let them come and go.

You can recognize that your thoughts are nothing more than an ever-changing stream of words, sounds and pictures, as opposed to what they can appear to be – threatening, upsetting truths and facts.

One way to defuse from your thoughts is as described under the heading 'Let go' a few pages back: to imagine your thoughts as, for example, helium balloons floating away.

Another way to defuse from your thoughts is to imagine the thought as words on a Karaoke screen. Suppose, for example, you often think to yourself 'I'm boring', 'I never have anything interesting to say' or 'I'm not as clever as most people.' Imagine those thoughts as words on a Karaoke screen. Then, visualize a bouncing ball jumping from word to word. Or imagine the thoughts in the voice of a cartoon character, or sing it to the tune of 'Happy Birthday'.

The idea, then, is not to try and get rid of your thoughts, but simply to learn how to step back and see them for what they are – just words, phrases and ideas that are passing through. Your relationship with the thought has changed – it can be seen as just words.

Identifying your values and committing to action

Once you've accepted and then detached yourself from your negative, anxious thoughts, the next step is to *do* something. You use a 'beginner's mind': you start afresh, focus and engage. You do things that are guided by your values.

Your values represent what's important and has some worth to you. Examples of values might be connecting with others, having meaningful friendships, being reliable, having fun, and being authentic and genuine.

Anxious thoughts drive you into doing things that you don't really want to do. Your values, on the other hand, represent what you'd rather be guided by. Your values are a truer reflection of who you really are.

Values propel you forward and give you goals and purpose even while anxiety is present. You can allow anxious thoughts to be there but don't let them stop you from doing the things you value.

So if, for example, being able to pick up your children from school every day is important to you, or being a reliable employee is important to you, you allow anxious feelings to be there even if it's difficult or uncomfortable, but you turn up at the playground or work each day anyway.

Understandably, you may think you have to get a handle on your anxiety before you can do *anything* constructive

– anything that you'd really like to do. However, ACT encourages you to 'commit to action.' You set goals according to your values and commit to fulfilling them. It requires courage: the ability to do what's important to you *despite* your fear and concerns.

Whether you want to leave your job or a relationship, attend an interview, go to a party or travel somewhere new, courage will help you be brave, grasp the nettle and move forward. Focus on what it is you want to achieve. Keeping that in your mind can help stop feelings of doubt, uncertainty and fear creeping in.

Wezi explains, 'It was important to me to be able to meet my children from school – to go to the playground, wait for them and walk them home. I accepted that I was going to feel anxious and I took it one step at a time; a friend came with me the first few times. I didn't go into the playground at first, I waited outside the school gate. I then progressed to going into the playground with my friend. A while later, I was able to do it on my own. It was scary but I managed.'

Be like Wezi: feel the fear and do it anyway!

In a nutshell

• With mindfulness, you focus on what you *can* manage and control, now in the present moment. This can really help you to feel calmer, more in control and able to manage.

- The mindful qualities of awareness, acknowledgement, acceptance, being non-judgemental and letting go can help you to be aware of when you're getting caught up in anxious thoughts and feelings and to know that thoughts are simply 'mental events' that do not have to have control over you.
- The mindful qualities of beginner's mind, patience, focus and engagement can help you to slow down, gain a sense of perspective, think positively and feel more capable of managing situations and events.
- Acceptance and Commitment Therapy (ACT) is one of the recent mindfulness-based behaviour therapies and coaching models that can be effective in managing anxiety.
- Acceptance and Commitment Therapy involves learning to *accept* what may be out of your personal control, identifying your values and *committing* to action that will improve your life.
- It requires courage: the ability to do what's important to you *despite* your fear and concerns.

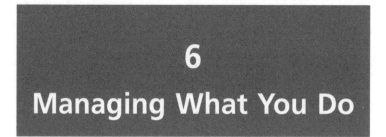

6
Managing What You Do

Some people are quite aware of the links between their anxious thoughts and the feelings and behaviour that accompany those thoughts. James, for example, knows that when he has to attend a meeting at work, he's likely to feel stressed and tense a couple of days beforehand and he usually suffers from a low-level migraine.

Other people know they are thinking anxious thoughts but any physical symptoms they experience – digestive problems, headaches, tension in their shoulders, for example – they view as something quite separate and don't link them to being anxious. If they have a physical symptom, they think it means they have a separate physical problem. And that can just add to their worries and fears.

Other people may be *only* aware of the physical symptoms and not even recognize they've been anxious about something or a number of things.

Erin, for example, explains how, for six months she experienced stomach aches and digestive problems, and was constantly going to the loo. 'I was afraid I had a serious stomach disorder – an ulcer or a tumour. I felt unable to explain how I felt to my partner or a close friend and I was reluctant to go to my GP. Finally, I made an appointment and after a long consultation, my doctor worked out that the last 12 months had actually been very stressful at work and with family problems. I also had a lot coming up in the next few months that I knew I had to deal with. My physical symptoms – the stomach problems – were caused by a general anxiety disorder. I just didn't realize how anxious I'd been.'

But remember, anxiety has physical and behavioural aspects as well as cognitive aspects, and each aspect can trigger another. Your thoughts can create physical sensations. If you were to think about eating a thin slice of lemon, for example, your mouth would probably start watering. If you see someone yawning, you may find yourself doing the same. If you look at an erotic picture, then your body will respond to that too.

In the same way, anxiety is not 'all in your head'. Anxiety is experienced throughout your body as well. So, part of managing anxiety involves managing the physical aspects – in appropriate, constructive ways. In fact, you might find that, for many situations, changing what you do may be easier or more practical than changing how and what you think. And once you manage the physical feelings, the thoughts slow down and become calmer – more rational and reasonable.

We've all experienced the physical feelings that come with anxiety: a racing heart, for example, feeling hot and cold, butterflies in the stomach, 'wired' feelings of tension, feeling faint, nausea, trembling and so on. There are many different ways in which people experience physical anxiety, but they are all related to our 'fight or flight' response.

How/why worry and anxiety affect your body

When a problem, difficulty or challenge presents itself, your body gets prepared to deal with it. The fight or flight response causes your body's nervous system to release hormones such as adrenaline and cortisol. These hormones can boost blood sugar levels and triglycerides (blood fats) which the body can use immediately for fuel to fight or flee a dangerous situation.

All well and good. However, when you're anxious, if you think things like, 'I'll get horribly lost' or 'What if I make a mistake on this project?' you're scaring yourself with your thoughts of danger and disaster, and your body responds by creating the symptoms associated with fear and stress.

When the excessive fuel in the blood isn't used for physical activities, the hormone surges, rapid heartbeat, shallow breathing and muscle tension can lead to more long-term symptoms such as:

- Trembling, twitching and tingling;
- Headaches;
- Muscle tension and aches;

- Clenched jaw;
- Digestive problems;
- Irritability and inability to concentrate;
- Nervous energy;
- Tiredness and fatigue.

If you persistently suffer from these symptoms, it's important to see a doctor to rule out unrelated physical problems. And if the physical symptoms do appear to be a result of anxiety, there is, of course, medication available to manage the physical effects. Some of the most common medications for long-term treatment of anxiety are antidepressants known as selective serotonin reuptake inhibitors, or SSRIs, which work by restoring the balance of chemicals in the brain. Sertraline and paroxetine are examples of SSRIs commonly used to treat anxiety disorders.

Anxiety attacks may also be treated with quick-acting medications like diazepam (Valium) or another benzodiazepine, useful for short-term treatment of severe panic attacks.

Anxiety and its physical side effects may be managed with beta blockers, which are usually used to treat heart conditions and high blood pressure. Beta blockers like propanolol slow the heart rate and relax blood vessels, which can ease physical symptoms.

You may try to deal with the symptom that bothers you the most yourself. For example, if you experience digestive stress because of anxiety, you may take over-the-counter stomach medication; if you suffer from headaches, you might take painkillers from the chemist, and so on.

They may or may not help. There are, though, other things you can do to manage the physical effects of anxiety.

Acknowledge and accept

Start by being aware that you are experiencing a physical symptom of anxiety; experience and observe it without either fixating on it or reacting to it as if it's an emergency situation. Take a mindful approach (see Chapter 5) and accept that whatever the reason and however difficult, 'wrong' or 'ridiculous' it might seem, you do feel like you do.

Bring down the physical feelings

Having acknowledged and accepted the physical sensations you experience, you can then dial down the physical feelings.

Your way of breathing has a direct influence on your physical symptoms. When you're in danger, in an emergency, instead of breathing at a normal rate you start to breathe rapidly and shallowly from your upper lungs, you hyperventilate – taking in more air than your body needs.

If you don't respond to the potential danger with fight or flight, then you may experience the uncomfortable symptoms that accompany anxiety, fear or panic: feeling light-headed, dizziness, confusion, shortness of breath, tingling or numbness in the hands or feet, feelings of nausea.

The good news is that by changing your breathing you can reverse these symptoms. By managing your breathing, the following happens:

- Your need for oxygen decreases;
- Your breathing slows;
- Your heart rate slows;
- Your blood pressure decreases;
- Your muscle tension decreases;
- You begin to feel more at ease and calm.

It's useful to know, though, that there's a difference between getting het up and calming back down. The difference is in the timing. The 'emergency reaction' is instant: all those physical changes – rapid heartbeat, fast, shallow breathing and so on – all happen together, instantly. It takes longer, though, for your body to 'come down'. But although it does take a while for the body to respond to a calming response, you *can* make it happen.

It can really help you to dial down the physical feelings if you can learn to manage your breathing. It might be advice you've heard before, but it really can help.

Learn a natural breathing technique that gives you sufficient oxygen and controls the exhalation of carbon dioxide. It's very simple and it goes like this:

Gently and slowly breathe in through your nose. Breathe in a little bit deeper than you normally would. Then, exhale through your mouth with your lips slightly and gently pursed together. Count to three as you exhale. Continue this breathing pattern for several minutes until you feel calmer.

This way of breathing is the opposite of that which comes automatically during anxious moments.

Concentrating on your breathing does two things: as well as slowing everything down – your rapid heartbeat and your racing thoughts – it can slow down or distract your mind and give it something helpful to think about. It's mindful; when you focus on your breathing you are focusing on something that is happening now, in the present. It helps to anchor, or ground, you.

Of course, you may notice thoughts arising as you breathe. Just allow them to come and go and return your focus and attention to your breathing.

Managing your breathing also has the benefit of being a simple thing you can do anywhere, any time. You can practise it any time too – remind yourself by writing the word 'breathe' on a sticky note and stick it on your computer, near the phone or on the fridge to remind you to slow down and simply breathe.

There are a number of other ways to manage your breathing. I've described them below. Try them out and see which one you prefer – which feels the most doable for you? Which breathing technique you use is not as important as just remembering to use one of them!

Feel your breathing

Feel your breathing. Place one hand on your chest and feel your breath moving into and out of your body. Notice the natural rhythm. Be aware of the coolness of the air as you breathe in and the warmth of the air leaving you as you exhale.

Count your breathing

Breathe and count forwards and backwards. Start by counting up to 7 as you breathe in, and then back down from 7 as you breathe out; then count to 6 as you breathe in, and back from 6 as you breathe out. Continue like this till you get to 3 and then return to counting up to 7. As you get down to the lower numbers, count more slowly.

Imagine your breathing

Use your imagination. Breathe in like you're taking in the scent of a flower. Breathe out like you're blowing bubbles. Imagine that your breaths are just like the ocean waves: they come and they go. Or, imagine breathing out to the ends of the universe and breathing from there back into your body. Or breathe colour; imagine the colour of the air filling not just your lungs but your entire body.

Know that when you manage your breathing – a physical aspect – you will also be managing your thoughts and behaviour: the cognitive and behavioural aspects of worry and anxiety.

Trust your body's ability to breathe

What if it's breathing itself that's causing you problems?

When you're anxious, you might experience a tight sensation in your chest or throat. It's just your chest and throat muscles that are tense, but the feeling can make you believe that you're not getting enough air. This can then lead to panic and light-headedness, feeling you're not getting enough oxygen or that you could stop breathing altogether.

Before you know it, a cycle of anxiety begins as one fear feeds off the other. What to do?

Even though it might feel like it, you are not actually going to stop breathing. You can prove this to yourself by taking a deep breath and holding it for as long as possible. After holding your breath for however long, your body will reach a point where it automatically prompts you to release quickly and breathe in. As always, your breathing will, at some point, return to normal. Remember that!

Doing this exercise can help you to feel more confident in your body's ability to breathe. You'll know that whatever you do with your breathing, your body is always in control and always looks after your breathing for you.

However, if you find that focusing on your breathing just makes things worse – that whenever you're worried, *whatever* you focus on becomes an issue – then don't think about your breathing at all. Acknowledge and try to accept it; if you feel that your breathing is too rapid and shallow, then allow it to be rapid and shallow.

Instead, you might want to try doing something physical.

Get up and get moving: exercise and physical activity

Remember, when you're feeling worried, anxious or fearful your body releases stress hormones, such as adrenaline and cortisol. These contribute towards the physical symptoms that you experience, such as a racing pulse. If there's nothing you can actually do about the cause of your anxiety – if you don't use your stress hormones up in 'fight or flight' – then those hormones can keep you feeling agitated for quite some time.

Doing something physical can really help.

> 'I've always found that running helps me. I think of exercise as a proactive thing to do for my own well-being. If I'm feeling agitated, stressed or wired, I get out and run. It's difficult to hang onto anxious thoughts when I'm running. When I finish I always feel calmer.'

Physical activity uses up adrenaline, relieves the tension and can distract you from those worrying thoughts. Certainly, running, playing football or tennis and other fitness activities can help. But it doesn't have to be an organized sport or structured exercise programme.

Any physical activity – gardening, washing your car, housework or simply walking briskly around the block – that gets you up and moving can help.

As well as relieving tension and using up adrenaline, exercise is a good way to help keep worries from overwhelming you, because it can change the focus from your mind to your body.

Of course, when you're feeling worried or anxious, exercise can feel like the last thing you want to do. But once you get going you may find it really can make a difference, easing symptoms of anxiety and helping you feel better.

If you like being outdoors, run, walk, cycle, do some gardening, play ball or throw the dog a ball. Walking, running, cycling and swimming allow you to be active at your own pace and you can do them alone. But you might want to ask a friend to join you – you might prefer the company.

Get active in your way. Do it at your own pace and ability. What could you do? Think of two or three physical activities that, because you can do or like doing them, you'll be more likely to do when you need to use up your anxious energy.

As well as using up the adrenaline and other hormones and allowing muscles to relax, physical activity and exercise release feel-good brain chemicals: endorphins.

> 'I like walking. I find getting out in the country for a walk and to stop, sit and look at a view, helps with perspective. I feel calmer.'

Walking is good – anyone can do it at any age and any fitness level. It's good for your heart, your head and your wallet! Walking is also a great way to connect with nature. Research shows that walking in green spaces – the park or the countryside – reduces stress levels, improves mood, enhances psychological well-being and improves attention and concentration.

You can walk on your own or with other people and it doesn't cost a thing. Websites such as www.meetup.com have walking groups.

If you can't get outside, find an exercise DVD or YouTube film that you can follow. Or do some housework – vacuum, clean the windows, the bathroom, change the bed linen or make the bed.

Whatever you do, it will also be a distraction that can get you away from the cycle of negative thoughts that feed anxiety.

What you eat

If you're worried and anxious, how and what you eat affects how you and your stomach feel.

Greasy, fried foods, fatty foods and rich sauces can make you feel queasy. Alcohol, coffee and high sugar content foods can leave you feeling wired. Avoiding these foods is unlikely to cure anxiety, but it will help.

If you suffer from Irritable Bowel Syndrome, managing your diet will help with the symptoms.

However, there is no one specific diet for people with the condition. What works best for you will depend on your symptoms and how you react to different foods when you're worried and anxious.

Whatever your symptoms, it may help to:

- Have regular meals – don't skip meals or leave gaps between meals;
- Take your time when eating – don't rush;
- Drink plenty of water and/or non-caffeinated drinks, such as herbal tea;
- Restrict the amount of tea, coffee, alcohol and fizzy drinks you drink.

Finally, when you feel anxiety in your stomach, do try some of the breathing techniques, physical activities and exercises mentioned in this chapter. They really can help relieve the symptoms of a 'dodgy tummy.'

In a nutshell

- Anxiety is not 'all in your head', it's experienced throughout your body as well.
- You may or may not be aware that your anxious thoughts are related to your physical feelings or that physical symptoms are related to being anxious.
- Changing what you do may actually be easier or more practical for you than changing how and what you think.
- People experience physical anxiety in different ways and they are all related to our 'fight or flight' response.
- If you persistently suffer from physical symptoms, it's important to see a doctor to rule out unrelated physical problems.
- Your way of breathing has a direct influence on your physical symptoms. By managing your breathing you can reverse these symptoms.
- When you're anxious, the physical changes – rapid heartbeat, fast, shallow breathing and so on – all happen together, instantly. It takes longer, though, for your body to 'come down.'
- Trust your body's ability to breathe. Know that whatever you do with your breathing, your body is always in control and always looks after your breathing for you.
- Doing something physical can really help you manage the physical symptoms that have been triggered by your anxiety.

- Any physical activity – sport, exercise, housework, cleaning the car or gardening – that gets you up and moving can help.
- When you're feeling worried or anxious, exercise can feel like the last thing you want to do. Get active your way. Do it at your own pace and ability.

7
Using Solution-Based Problem Solving

Just as we each have different thoughts and physical feelings when we are anxious, we each behave in different ways too.

If you were feeling anxious because you were waiting for a phone call, email or letter to tell you whether or not you'd been offered the job, you might pace up and down the room. Someone else might sit and bite their nails. Someone else might chain smoke or stuff their face with cake. Someone else might carry out some ritualistic behaviours: counting or checking things, for example.

How we each behave when we're anxious or worried depends on a variety of things, including what has triggered the anxiety, our ability to manage the situation and how the situation relates to our past experiences.

Perhaps you avoid situations that have made you feel anxious in the past and you also avoid similar activities and situations that you expect will make you more anxious.

These are known as 'avoidance behaviours': the things people do or don't do to reduce the risk of feeling anxious.

Avoidance behaviours can involve 'doing' or 'not doing' things. 'Doing' behaviours might be ritualistic and compulsive behaviours such as excessively washing hands, wearing 'safe' clothes, counting or checking. They might involve dependency behaviours: depending on, for example, other people, alcohol or medication to help you avoid anxious thoughts and feelings.

An example of a 'not doing' behaviour is when a person avoids leaving their home in order to try to avoid panicky feelings.

When total avoidance is not possible, you may resort to escape behaviours: leaving or escaping in the middle of a situation. For example, if you couldn't actually avoid or get out of a social situation, you might find a way to leave as soon as you possibly could.

One of the problems with avoidance behaviours is that they actually keep you in a fearful state. For example, supposing you avoid a social situation at the last minute because of your anxious thoughts and feelings. You get to the door and your anxiety increases. You turn around and go home.

Once you're home, your physical feelings subside: your breathing rate returns to normal, your heart rate starts to slow down and your temperature returns to normal. In other words, your body reinforces your avoidance. Your body relaxes and tells you that you did the right thing.

You feel a sense of relief and comfort as you tell yourself, 'Thank goodness I didn't go in. What if I had? My heart would have raced so strongly that I would have had a panic attack. I'd have made a fool of myself.'

The reduction of your physical symptoms, along with your thoughts about what would've happened if you had gone to the party will reinforce your decision to avoid similar social situations in future.

But ask yourself: how much of your time and mental energy has avoidance coping sucked up? How has it affected your relationships with family, friends and colleagues? How has it affected your self-esteem and confidence?

Avoidance behaviours are simply a crutch – they provide temporary, and inappropriate, relief. The problem is, avoidance behaviours trick you into believing that you've successfully solved the problem of whatever it is that triggers your anxiety.

While avoidance may make you feel better in the short term, you never get the chance to learn how to cope with your fears and take control of situations. It either doesn't occur to you that there must be a better way to respond or if it does, you don't know how to *constructively* resolve what's worrying you. But *facing* your fears is the key. You can do this with a technique known as 'solution-focused problem solving'. It involves focusing on what you can change, rather than aspects of the situation that are beyond your control. You spend your time and energy focusing on solutions, not the problems.

Solution-focused problem solving

Start by noticing and accepting your anxious thoughts and feelings. If you need reminding about the process of acceptance, turn back to Chapter 5 on mindfulness to remind yourself about this.

Noticing and accepting your symptoms will serve as the foundation for the next steps. When you are having trouble applying new skills, think first about whether you are applying the principle of acceptance.

If you can accept your anxious thoughts and feelings, you give your neocortex – the rational part of your mind – the opportunity to start working for you.

It's useful to remember that when you're anxious and get more het up about feeling anxious, the highly reactive limbic part of your brain takes over and your neocortex – the thinking part of your brain – shuts down.

Instead of allowing initial worries to prompt you to find a constructive solution to whatever you're worried about, when you're anxious, you've allowed those worries to grow and overwhelm your mind.

The first step, then, is to calm down the anxiety-provoking amygdala in your limbic brain and engage the neocortex: the thinking part of your brain. It takes effort, practice and a commitment to calm down, but you can do this.

You can further engage the thinking part of your brain by giving it something simple and neutral to think about. It could simply be remembering what you had to eat for each meal yesterday. Or you could try counting backwards from 50 or reciting the alphabet backwards or reciting the lyrics to your favourite song or poem. It might be answering a few clues in a crossword puzzle.

It could be using one of the breathing techniques in Chapter 6. Breathing techniques can be useful to 'bring yourself down' so that you can begin to think straight.

Don't make it so hard a task, though, that you give up and let your mind revert to your worries.

Once you feel like you're more able to think straight, you can start tackling whatever is worrying you and making you anxious.

Learn to plan instead of worry

There's no doubt that worrying can be helpful when it spurs you to take action and solve a problem. But worrying on its own doesn't improve a situation. Getting into a cycle of worry and anxiety will not help you think clearly or help you to deal with a potential problem.

You need to take action: positive, constructive, helpful action. Address the problem, make some changes and see some progress. Then you'll feel more in control and less worried. You'll have moved from creating problems to solving problems.

In Chapter 5 you will have read about an aspect of mindfulness known as 'beginner's mind': being open to new possibilities and identifying what you can do differently.

Taking a beginner's mind approach means that whatever you're worried about – especially if it's something you've been worried about before and it turned out badly – you know that you *can* make it different from last time.

Although it might appear to be counter-intuitive advice, it can actually help if you start by identifying and acknowledging what the worst case scenario would be. Why? Because once you've acknowledged what it is you fear happening, then you know exactly what it is that you're up against. You can then move on to what your options are to minimize or manage the worst case scenario.

For example, if you were worried about driving somewhere new, your worst case scenario could be that you would get lost, drive around in circles and maybe even run out of petrol.

A worst case scenario with a looming deadline at work is that you won't meet the deadline, your manager will be angry and everyone else will think you're incompetent.

Or, in another example, you might be going to a party where you don't know anyone. The worst case scenario is that you end up in a corner on your own with no one to talk to and have a panic attack.

What are *you* worried about right now? What's the worst that could happen?

Whatever it is, you can learn to plan instead of worry. Worry involves your mind going over and over the same problems. A plan, though, gives you a positive focus.

There are six steps to take:

1. Identify the specific problem and the worst case scenario.
2. Identify the best case scenario.
3. Identify options and possible solutions.
4. Choose one of the options or solutions.
5. Break your solution down into manageable steps.
6. Review the outcome.

1. Identify the specific problem and the worst case scenario

So, the first thing to ask yourself is, 'What's the problem and what's the worst that could happen?'

Write your answer down. Try to be as specific as possible. For example:

- 'We're in debt; we owe money. We could lose the house.'
- 'I've got a deadline. If I don't meet it my manager will be angry and use it against me.'
- 'I won't know anyone at the party. I'll feel stupid. I won't know how to leave without appearing rude. I'll have a panic attack.'

2. Identify the best case scenario

Next, identify what you would really like to happen: what the best case scenario would be. This is a similar approach to 'Identifying your values and committing to action' – the aspect of Acceptance and Commitment Therapy (see Chapter 5) that involves working out what's important to you and doing something that will help you, based on what's important.

Think about what you would like the outcome to be. For example, with the work deadline, would you like the outcome to be that you are able to meet it? Or would you prefer that the deadline is extended and you have more time?

When you're anxious, you can lose sight of what it is you want; you're too busy thinking about what you *don't* want. Knowing what you want and where you want to get to makes a successful outcome much more likely – because you have a positive focus.

3. Identify options and possible solutions
Once you've decided what you would like to happen, think of a couple of things you could do – positive, constructive things – that might help you achieve the best case scenario.

Don't feel that you have to find a perfect solution. Just identify what you *can* change, rather than aspects of the situation that are beyond your control.

With a work deadline, for example, the options might be to:

* Ask someone to help you;
* Work overtime to get it finished on time;
* Identify what the key parts are that need completing on time and which parts can be handed in later;
* Negotiate with your manager for more time.

Another example might be that you are anxious about telling a friend or family member that you don't want them to come and visit. What are your options here? They might include:

- Just phone and cancel;
- Send a text or email saying, 'I'm not going to be able to have you visit this weekend. Could you phone so I can explain?';
- Suggest another date;
- Suggest a different way to get together.

Don't worry about how unrealistic an idea seems. Write down anything and everything. The idea here is simply to generate some possibilities. It may help to consider:

- What, if anything, you've done before in a similar situation that was genuinely helpful (not an avoidance strategy though!) that you could use again.
- What, if anything, you've done before in a similar situation that was *not* helpful. What did you learn that you can use to make the next experience a better one?
- What ideas and solutions your friends or family would suggest. This doesn't mean to say you'd take their advice, but just thinking about what they might advise could be useful.
- What have other people who have faced similar worries and anxieties done? Ask them. Listen to how they coped.

All of these will give you some ideas. This process of identifying your options will stretch you beyond your usual way of thinking and behaving.

Be sure to write your ideas, options and solutions down, so that you can actually see them. Writing things down can really help this process for a couple of reasons. Firstly, writing them down forces you to define more clearly what your options are. Secondly, rather than trying to keep them in your head, writing your ideas and options down externalizes your ideas – you can actually see them.

Turn your mind to positive possibilities and remind yourself that you *can* make it different from last time. (This is why training your brain to think positively is so helpful – it will help you and make it easier to look for positive possibilities when you're identifying new options.)

> 'I'd been so worried about my money problems but once I had written down my options, I felt a huge sense of relief. I felt I was taking control. Even if there were setbacks, I still felt it was going to be possible to be debt-free at some point in the future. I felt hopeful.'

4. Choose one of the options or solutions

Once you've written down some options, choose a solution from the options you've identified. Which actions or solutions feel right to you? Would it be helpful to go through reasons 'for' and 'against' each idea?

If you're still unsure, don't add to your worries by trying to find the perfect solution. Over thinking can lead to confusion and paralyse you, so that you end up with no decision. (And yet making no decision is still a decision; you've made a decision not to do anything!)

When the situation allows it, stepping away for a bit can help you see things with fresh eyes and a fresh mind when you come back to it.

Don't wait, though, until you feel completely certain about something before you take action. The sooner you can do something, the sooner you'll feel more confident, in control and less worried.

Just know that you might never know for sure the outcome of a certain action, but you can always prepare yourself to deal with the possible obstacles or challenges that arise.

5. Break your solution down into manageable steps

To make things feel easier and more manageable, you will need to break your chosen solution down into smaller steps. The number of steps required will vary depending on the situation.

So, supposing you were concerned about attending a party: that you'll not know anyone, not know what to say to people, feel stupid. The worst case scenario is that you'll have a panic attack. The best case scenario is that you'll feel reasonably calm, chat to a few people and then come home feeling good about it all.

The solution you chose was to go to the party and ask a friend to come with you.

The steps might include;

- Ask the person whose party it is about the other people who are going to the party – see if you share any common interests with anyone else there.
- Be honest with the friend you've asked to come with you; ask them to include you in conversations with others.

- Remind yourself to breathe and focus on positive self-talk.
- Decide how much time you will spend at the party and make sure you can leave when you decide to leave – that transport is available.

These steps work together to make a plan. Once you have a plan with positive, manageable steps, combined with hopeful, positive thoughts about the event, breathing techniques, acceptance of your anxious feelings, etc. you're more likely to manage.

If, at any point, you find yourself worrying again, tell yourself, 'Stop! I have a plan!' Remind yourself of the steps you are going to take and keep your thoughts on that.

What things would you usually avoid because they make you anxious? Start small – take small steps. Start with something that would not be too challenging. It doesn't matter if they are very small steps; the aim is to enable you to regain enough sense of control to feel that, little by little, you can move forward. Even the smallest actions are steps in the right direction.

Visualize a positive outcome – create images for yourself where you see yourself coping and achieving successful outcomes. Instead of playing out the worst scenario in your mind, you play out the best.

The more you imagine yourself coping and coming out the other side, the more likely it is to happen. Remember, seeing yourself coping makes your brain believe that it is, indeed, possible.

6. Review the outcome

Once you've been through the situation – attended the party, driven somewhere new, dealt with the work deadline, for example – review the outcome. What worked? What went well? What helped it to go well? If it didn't go as well as you would've liked, what did you learn? What would you do differently next time?

Exposure: gradually and repeatedly facing your fears

An approach to a solution-focused plan is to open yourself to what makes you anxious, in a safe and controlled way. This is known as 'desensitization' or 'exposure': you gradually and repeatedly expose yourself to what makes you anxious and you gradually overcome the anxiety and fear.

The ACT approach of acceptance (described in Chapter 5) is a form of exposure: you expose yourself to anxious thoughts and feelings and learn to accept them.

With exposure, whatever it is that triggers your anxiety, each time you expose yourself to it, you feel a little bit more confident and in control. The anxious feelings begin to lose their power.

If you've tried this in the past and it didn't work, you may have started with something too big. Rather than try exposure with a situation that completely overwhelms you, it's important to begin with a situation that you feel you could handle and work your way up from there, building your confidence and coping skills.

As an example, let's look at how Joelle overcame her anxiety about crossing a bridge. Here are the steps she took:

Step one: Look at pictures of bridges.
Step two: Look at pictures of someone else crossing a bridge.
Step three: Watch someone else crossing a bridge.
Step four: Cross a low bridge with a friend.
Step five: Cross the low bridge on your own.
Step six: Cross a higher bridge with a friend.
Step seven: Cross the higher the bridge on your own.

At every step, Joelle acknowledged and accepted her feelings, managed her breathing and focused on positive thoughts. She didn't move on to the next step until she'd practised her current step a number of times.

Take your own steps

If there's something you'd like to overcome that makes you feel anxious, make a list of small steps you could take. Arrange the steps from the least anxiety-provoking to the most scary. It can be helpful to think about your end goal – for example, instead of walking the long way round to get to work each day, to be able to cross a bridge to get there – and then break down the steps needed to reach that goal.

Start with the first step (in this example, looking at pictures of bridges) and don't move on until you start to feel more comfortable doing it. When feelings of anxiety or panic arise, try and accept them and remember to avoid 'fusing' with your thoughts.

Stay in the situation long enough for your anxiety to decrease. The longer you expose yourself to the thing you're afraid of, the more you'll get used to it and the less anxious you'll feel when you face it the next time.

If the situation itself is short – for example, crossing a bridge – do it over and over again until your anxiety starts to lessen. Once you've taken a step on several separate occasions without feeling too much anxiety, you can move on to the next step. If a step is too hard, break it down into smaller steps or go more slowly.

The aim is to build your confidence – with each step to believe that you can do it and to feel more calm and capable.

Practise
It's important to practise regularly. Practise often but go at a pace that you can manage without feeling over-whelmed. With each step, you will experience anxiety, but remember to acknowledge and accept those feelings. Breathe. Talk yourself down. Focus on positive thoughts and images.

Review the outcome
As you go through each step, review the outcome. What worked? What helped and went well? If it didn't go as well as you would've liked, identify what you would do differ-ently next time. What could be improved?

Reward yourself
With each step you achieve, reinforce your success by treating yourself to something. It could just be a cup of tea and a piece of cake. Whatever makes you happy.

Many phobias are successfully managed and cured using this method of exposure and desensitization. Simple phobias can be treated through gradual exposure to the object, animal, place or situation that causes fear and anxiety. Treating complex phobias often takes longer. Professional support involving a talking therapy, such as Cognitive Behavioural Therapy, can be very helpful.

Go with the 'flow'

What if you've made a plan but can't put it into action right away? The party or the car journey isn't until next week, for instance, or the opportunity to ask your manager to extend the work deadline isn't possible until after the weekend?

Or it might be that what's worrying you is something that's not in your control – perhaps you're waiting to hear from a family member that they have arrived safely at their destination, for example, or you're waiting for the results of an exam or a medical test.

Dwelling on worst case scenarios is not going to help. Don't sit and quietly concentrate on your worries. You need to put those worrying thoughts aside and do something else. In other words, you need to distract yourself.

This is not about avoidance or escape. The idea is simply to divert your mind to something more pleasant that will engage you and will give you a break from worrying.

It involves accepting what is out of your control and instead focusing on something you enjoy and are good at. Something constructive (not destructive, like smoking and drinking) that will occupy your mind so well that there's no time or room for anxious thoughts.

It needs to be something you find interesting and that absorbs you, as such things are easier for you to focus on for sustained periods of time.

Think of times when you have been so absorbed in what you were doing that time passed without you realizing. It could've been a good book or a film, maybe it was when you were baking a cake, doing a puzzle, fixing or mending something. Whatever it was, as you did it, no other thoughts entered your mind because you became completely caught up in what you were doing. In fact, you probably didn't even notice the time that was passing.

This state of mind is known as 'flow'. A mind in a state of flow is so engaged there is no room for worrying, anxious thoughts.

Identify for yourself activities that you can turn to when you want to switch off from worrying; find something that you can dip into for ten minutes or immerse yourself in for an hour. Something that keeps you focused and engaged; not so difficult that it's stressful and you give up, but not so easy that you get bored, otherwise your mind will just revert to anxious thoughts.

It could be a riveting novel, a crossword or Sudoku or jigsaw puzzle, a game of tennis or a series of yoga sequences – anything that makes it difficult for your mind to wander off or for anxious thoughts to find their way into your head.

'The times I feel most alive are when I'm caught up in something that makes me forget myself. Art. Work. People. Nature.'

Donald Miller

Here are some ideas:

Team sports: Tennis, badminton, netball or football, whatever it is, there's no time to worry because the next shot is coming right at you!

Yoga, Tai Chi, swimming, judo, rock climbing, juggling: Each individual movement encourages your mind to engage and focus on the next move.

Singing and dancing to music: Sing and dance along to your favourite tunes in the kitchen. Being immersed in the music can divert your thoughts and lift your mood.

Creative interests: Gardening, drawing, painting, colouring books, decorating, renovating furniture, baking. Whatever it is, a creative activity is an enjoyable, constructive way to distract yourself from anxious thoughts.

Games and puzzles: Whether it's card and board games, computer games, jigsaws, crosswords or Sudoku, all require a level of concentration and provide a challenge that will have you totally absorbed.

Books, films and TV series: It could be a gripping thriller, science fiction or a clever comedy. Whatever the genre, as events unfold, you become lost in the story.

Laughter: Humour is an effective, simple way to distract your mind from worrying, anxious thoughts. It also provides a physical release of tension. Humorous stories and the depiction of different situations can help provide a different, lighter perspective.

It's relatively easy to access humour in your everyday life and to use it as a means of distracting yourself. Funny movies, comedy shows and videos are easily available through various media outlets. Entire television channels such as 'Dave' and 'Comedy Central' are devoted to humour.

Develop spirituality: Spirituality is about a sense of being part of something bigger, more eternal. It involves an awareness of – and relationship with – something that connects you to a purpose in life larger than yourself. Although spirituality can be part of a particular religion – in the way that most religions emphasize a connection with a greater reality – it can also be seen as being distinct from religion.

You can choose to define what spirituality means for yourself, in whatever way feels most real and natural to you. Your own sense of spirituality can come from something as simple as the enormity of a star-filled sky. Or you may get a sense of connection from contemplating a beautiful sunset, the power of the sea or listening and singing to music.

It might be from being outdoors and being aware of the changing seasons. Or from being part of an organization such as Amnesty International – a global movement of more than 7 million people in over 150 countries who campaign to end abuses of human rights.

Connect with other people: Spend time with people whose company you enjoy (more about this in Chapter 9). You can also help yourself by helping other people. Kind acts and gestures free you from focusing on yourself and enable you to reach out to someone else.

Keep a note of the things you enjoy doing: hobbies, sports, interests. They are activities where you can experience a sense of flow; they keep you so absorbed that you get a break from anxious thoughts. They are also activities that you can do just to provide a balance in your life – not just to divert your mind from anxious thoughts, but to help prevent them from appearing in the first place.

Of course, it's still possible that, regardless of whatever you do to distract yourself, your mind may keep wandering back to your worries. But if a worrying thought does enter your mind, acknowledge it, let it pass and then return to what you were doing.

Realize that worrying is a choice and do something better with your time. You don't have to feed your worry. When you notice that worries are swirling in your head, focus on another activity.

In a nutshell

- How we each behave when we're anxious or worried depends on a variety of things, including what has triggered the anxiety, our ability to manage the situation and how the situation relates to our past experiences.
- The things you do or don't do to reduce the risk of feeling anxious are known as 'avoidance behaviours'.
- While avoidance may make you feel better in the short term, you don't learn how to cope with your fears and take control of situations.

- Facing your fears is the key. Spend your time and energy focusing on *solutions*, not the problems.
- You can learn to plan – which gives you a positive focus – instead of worry.
- 'Exposure' is a behavioural technique that involves gradually and repeatedly exposing yourself to what makes you anxious in order to gradually overcome the anxiety and fear.
- There are times when you do need to put worrying, anxious thoughts aside and do something else; you need to distract yourself – to divert your mind to something you enjoy.

8
Boosting Your Confidence, Courage and Assertiveness

Confidence is the very opposite of anxiety. When you are anxious, you're more likely to believe that things will turn out badly. When you are confident, you're more likely to believe that things will turn out well.

Confidence – self-confidence – is about having belief in yourself and your abilities and *believing* that you can cope and that events and experiences will turn out well.

Your confidence may be markedly low when you are anxious. As well as being low in confidence, anxiety also makes it difficult to be assertive – to know what you do and don't want and to feel strong and stand up for yourself. Being unable to be assertive can then undermine your self-esteem – your feelings of worth.

It's an unhelpful cycle, with each aspect feeding into the other: if you don't believe in yourself and your abilities, you probably find it difficult to assert yourself. Then, because you don't assert yourself in a range of situations, you feel bad about yourself. That just undermines your confidence further and you feel more anxious. And so on.

The good news is that this also works in reverse: building your confidence gives you the ability to be assertive and being more assertive helps you feel good about yourself. And if you feel good about yourself, you feel more confident about your abilities. You'll feel less anxious. It's a positive dynamic where, again, each aspect feeds into the other.

Start from a position of strength

The best place to start building your confidence is from a position of strength. This means identifying the area or areas of your life that are important to you and you do reasonably well in. It could be, for example, your work, hobbies and interests, sport, health and fitness. Or it could be religion, family and/or friends that are most important to you and are areas that you enjoy and feel most like yourself in.

Josh, for example, is 34. Sport is important to him – in particular, football is important. It's something he enjoys and does well in. He feels confident and good about himself when he plays football.

Whenever we enjoy and do well in an area of our life that's important to us, we can feel good about ourselves.

It could be caring for others, being a good friend, making or baking, being good at and enjoying a sport or physical activity.

Identifying what's important to you and what you enjoy combines two other approaches already explained in this book. Firstly, identifying what's important to you is the same approach as identifying your values and committing to action (described in Acceptance and Commitment Therapy in Chapter 5). Secondly, identifying what you enjoy, what you find interesting and what absorbs you is what gives you a sense of 'flow', as described in Chapter 7.

What do you like doing? What do you enjoy? Are there activities in your life that bring you a sense of satisfaction? Make yourself aware of what those activities are so that when you're feeling anxious and agitated, you can revert to them to help you feel grounded and connected.

Build your confidence with courage
Next, you need to give yourself opportunities to succeed and achieve in areas that you've either lost confidence in or you want to feel more confident in. This uses the same principles as the solution-focused approach and 'exposure' explained in Chapter 7. You identify something you'd like to be 'better' at and take small steps to achieve it.

Once again, you'll need to develop courage: the ability to do what's important to you *despite* your anxiety and fear. Focus on what it is you want to achieve. Keeping your goal in mind can help stop feelings of doubt, uncertainty and fear creeping in.

Each day there may be situations where you need to make a courageous choice: picking up a spider, making a phone call, attending an interview or speaking up for yourself.

Whatever it is, courage is what makes you brave and helps overcome anxiety.

Tap into your courage. Think of a situation when you felt worried or anxious about doing something, yet you did it anyway and things turned out OK. What helped you to have courage? Next time you want to overcome your anxiety in a particular situation, remember that time and tap into your courage again.

Do one thing every day that scares you a little and feel your confidence and courage grow.

Take something that makes you anxious – maybe it's telling someone at work that you don't agree with their opinions or ways of doing things. Start with a small step: practise disagreeing by doing it with someone who doesn't scare you. For example, you could disagree with a good friend about their thoughts on a TV programme, book or film.

Making use of the techniques described in earlier chapters of this book – breathing techniques and positive self-talk, for example – can help support your courage.

Confident body language

Confidence and courage come through acting as if you are unafraid, even when you are. When you behave as if you are confident, other people assume that you are and they respond positively to you. This, in turn, helps you actually to feel confident.

Something that can really help you with this involves your body language.

Read the list of actions below and choose two that would feel most easy and natural for you to do:

- Stand or sit straight;
- Keep your head level;
- Relax your shoulders;
- Spread your weight evenly on both legs;
- If sitting, keep your elbows on the arms of your chair (rather than tightly against your sides);
- Make appropriate eye contact;
- Lower the pitch of your voice;
- Speak more slowly.

To support your confidence and courage, if you can use just one or two of these things consistently, your thoughts, feelings and the rest of your behaviour will catch up.

The good news is that you don't need to do all the actions on the list to feel and come across as confident. Instead, you only need to choose two actions. It's a dynamic process where small changes in how you use your body can add up to a big change in how you feel and, in turn, how you behave.

Assertiveness

Assertiveness doesn't come naturally or easily to many people, and it definitely doesn't feel natural or easy when you're feeling worried, anxious or scared. In many situations, when you're anxious it's tempting to keep quiet and say nothing. But being passive can actually increase your anxiety; you want to say something but you can't. And because what you want to say goes unspoken, stress and anxiety increase, making you more anxious.

Paul, for example, explains, 'I wanted to tell my mother-in-law to stop telling us how to manage our children. But because I was worried about how she'd respond, and how I'd deal with her response, I said nothing. But then, every time she was due to visit, I just got more anxious about her coming and the critical remarks she'd make.'

When you're in a situation where you need to assert yourself – for example, asking your brother not just to drop by, but to phone and arrange to visit, or telling a colleague you don't want to be a part of the team that is working on a project – anxiety can stop you in your tracks.

But don't confident, assertive people ever feel anxious about expressing their needs and wishes? Of course they do, but rather than focus on how worried and anxious they feel, they deal with these situations *despite* their fears and worries. They have courage.

Learning how to handle difficult situations and to assert yourself can make you feel more confident and, therefore, less anxious and worried.

What, though, does being assertive involve? It involves knowing what you do and don't want and being able to say so, clearly, directly and calmly. It means being able to express your feelings, thoughts, opinions and needs. It involves being able to assert your rights while at the same time taking into account the rights, needs and wishes of other people.

How to be assertive when you're anxious

Often, the mere thought of having to express yourself – to tell someone what you do or don't want – is enough to kick start anxiety: your mind starts racing and your stomach starts churning. You can't think straight and you just want to leave.

Even though you might be anxious, it *is* possible to be assertive. Start by being aware of how you feel. Acknowledge and accept those feelings. Breathe. Choose one or two of the confident body language actions described a couple of pages back.

Be clear and direct

Before you say anything, decide exactly what it is that you do or don't want. Also, decide just how far you're prepared to compromise and what your plan B might be if you don't get what you want.

You'll stay more focused on the conversation and less focused on how anxious you are if you can keep in mind what you do or don't want. For example, imagine you want to turn down a colleague who has asked you to be part of a team taking on a new piece of work. You're anxious about saying no. You think your colleague might pressure you and try to persuade you to agree.

Or, in another example, you want to tell your brother that you want him to phone you before he visits; that you don't want him just to turn up on your doorstep.

You'll need to be clear and direct; using hints or excuses can distort or weaken the meaning of what you really mean. So, simply say, 'I'm sorry, I'm going to say no to working on that project,' or, 'Before you call round to see me, I'd like you to phone first.'

Saying what you do or don't want in this way also reflects one of the key principles of Acceptance and Commitment Therapy – that of doing what's in keeping with your personal values, regardless of the feelings that may come up.

> 'In my teens and early twenties I used to get anxious about speaking my mind in a way which was true to myself, partly due to lack of confidence but also because I did not really know what I did and didn't want.
>
> However, over time and with a little help, I became aware of my values and what is important to me and started to express myself more truthfully. It wasn't easy, I can tell you, but I did it because, for me, it was the right thing to do.'

What if you're not sure what it is you do or don't want? Say so. Say, 'I'm not sure about this. I need some time to think about it and I'll get back to you.'

Acknowledge what the other person says, but stand your ground

Once you have said what you do or do not want, stop and listen to the other person's response. Then, before you reply, acknowledge their response. You do not have to agree with what the other person said, just be sure that you have understood. Calmly respond to the other person in a way that will both acknowledge you have understood what they've said but also confirm you are standing firm.

For example, to the colleague who wants you to work on the new project and tells you that they would really like you to be part of the team, 'Thanks for asking me, I understand you want me to be part of the team and you think I'd fit in well, but I'm not able to do it.' Or, to your brother, 'I understand that you think it's a nice surprise, but I'd really like you to phone me the day before you plan to call round.'

Negotiate and co-operate

Being assertive does not mean that you will always get what you want. It does mean, though, that you can start from a position of knowing what you feel and what you do and don't want. It also allows other people to state what they feel or want and, of course, they might want a different outcome!

Resist the urge to back down, argue or sulk. Instead, aim to negotiate or compromise with him or her. Aim for solutions and alternative courses of action.

For example, in the situation with your colleague, you *might* be prepared to offer to help in another way, 'I could talk to Roz and ask her if she can join you. We worked together on a similar project last year and she may well be able to join you. Shall I ask her?'

And to your brother, 'How about I let you know when I'm free the following week' or 'You could call me and we could meet for coffee, rather than you always coming round to me.'

Try and offer an alternative that works for you and benefits the other person as well. This way, you've neither given in nor insisted yours is the only way.

However, if you do choose to negotiate or compromise, bend as far as you can but no further. Know what your limits are and stand your ground.

Build confidence in your ability to be assertive

Start small: You don't have to launch into full-on assertiveness from the start. You can start by just adopting one step. For example, you might decide to start by accepting how you feel in situations where you could be assertive. Or you might choose to focus on acknowledging what the other person says. Once you feel comfortable with that, move on to another aspect of being assertive.

Practise: You could write down what you want to say and what the other person might say and read it aloud. Or, with a friend, rehearse the situation in which you plan to assert yourself. As well as thinking about what you're going to say, think about accepting how you might feel when you say it.

Focus on what went well: At some point after the conversation, write down one or two things that went well. Congratulate yourself!

What didn't go so well? Instead of obsessing about what didn't go well, think about what you would do differently in a similar situation in future.

How to say what you *do not* want – the key points:
- Notice how you feel;
- Ask for more information if you need it;
- If you don't want to do what the other person has asked, say no;
- Listen to and acknowledge the other person's response;
- Stand your ground and insist

Or

- Compromise and negotiate.

How to say what you *do* want – the key points:
- Identify how you feel and what, exactly, you want;
- Say what it is that you want;
- Listen to and acknowledge the other person's response;
- Stand your ground and stick to what you want; decide what your next step will be if you don't get what you want

Or

- Compromise and negotiate.

In a nutshell

- When you are anxious, you're more likely to believe that things will turn out badly. When you are confident, however, you're more likely to believe that things will turn out well.
- Start from a position of strength; if you can identify an area of your life that's important to you, that you enjoy and do well in, you are more likely to feel relatively good about yourself and your abilities.

- Make yourself aware of what those important activities are, so that when you're feeling agitated you can revert to them to help you feel grounded and connected.
- Identify something you'd like to be 'better' at and take small steps to achieve it.
- Build your confidence with courage: do what's important to you despite your anxiety and fear. Focus on what it is you want to achieve.
- Next time you want to overcome your anxiety in a particular situation, remember a time in the past when you overcame something you were anxious about, Tap into that courage again.
- Small changes in how you use your body can add up to a big change in how you feel.
- Learning how to handle difficult situations and to assert yourself can make you feel more confident and, therefore, less anxious and worried.
- Be clear about what you do or don't want and how far you're prepared to negotiate and compromise.

9
Finding Help and Support from Others

Talking to someone, such as a friend or family member, about anxiety and the effect it's having on you can help in a number of ways. It may help them to help you if they understand how you feel and what you experience. They may have experienced similar feelings and can share their experiences.

Voicing your worries can take away a lot of their scariness. Often, just having someone listen to you because they care can help.

If you can't talk to a partner, friend or family member – or if you do and they aren't helpful or you feel the need to talk things over with someone who is not directly involved in your life – your doctor, a counsellor or a support group (see the Other Useful Resources section at the back of this book) may help.

> 'Co-counselling workshops really helped me see things in a wider context.'

Positive people

How other people respond to you can make quite a difference to how you feel about yourself – to your confidence,
self-esteem and your ability to manage anxious thoughts
and feelings. You need positive people in your life.

Which people come to mind in the following list? Be creative in your thinking. The positive people on your list do
not necessarily have to be close friends or family, or people
you know. Maybe the person you can turn to in a crisis is
your GP or other health worker. Perhaps someone on television is the person who makes you laugh. The person
who inspires you could be someone you have read about
who has overcome adversity.

- Someone I can talk to if I am worried.
- Someone I can call on in a crisis.
- Someone who makes me feel good about myself.
- Someone I can totally be myself with.
- Someone who values my opinion.
- Someone who tells me how well I am doing.
- Someone who really makes me stop and think about
  what I am doing.
- Someone who makes me laugh.
- Someone who introduces me to new ideas, interests
  or new people.
- Someone who is spiritual: who has balance and a
  sense of perspective, a sense of wonder, who seeks
  out beauty and peace, who is interested in and con-
  cerned about others.

You may have a different person or a number of people
for each situation, or the same person for each and every

situation. Although having one positive person in your life can make all the difference to your ability to manage in these situations, do try and identify a few people who, in their different ways, could be your support network.

For every positive person out there, though, there is probably one negative person. Other people can be seen as 'radiators' or 'drains': radiators spread warmth and positivity, while drains take away your energy and resources, their negativity can increase your anxiety; just the thought of being around them can make you worried and anxious. They may, for example, be critical of you or just generally critical of everyone and everything. They may make fun of your anxiety or dismiss it and tell you you're being silly or ridiculous. (For additional guidance on this, you might be interested to read another of my books *How to Deal with Difficult People*, also published by Wiley.)

On the other hand, 'radiators' – positive people – are more likely to respond to you in a positive way. We all need 'radiators' in our lives; just being around 'radiators' can feel reassuring.

Of course, it's not always possible or practical to remove negative people from your life. What you can do, however, is spend less time around 'drains' and more time with 'radiators' – the positive people on your list.

Backing away from negative people also includes avoiding reading about other people who are portrayed as victims, where the focus is on the unfairness and suffering of their situation and problems never seem to get resolved. Stay away, too, from stories that judge, criticize and make fun of celebrities in tabloid papers, magazines and websites. Instead, look for stories about people who inspire you.

Read about people – ordinary people or famous people – who have coped with difficult times in their lives. What was it, do you think, that helped them manage? Their stories can inspire you and help you to think along positive lines.

Reach out and help other people

When you're worried, scared or anxious, it's easy to feel overwhelmed with your own concerns. But if you look beyond yourself and notice other people who are struggling in some way, you may find that your worries take a back seat. Help other people and, in the process, you help yourself; you bring a fresh perspective to your own life and circumstances.

> 'Develop the courage to think of others and to do something for them.'
>
> **Dalai Lama**

Studies show that even helping just one person can create feelings and attitudes that can lead to better physical health, better mental health and overall happiness.

Helping others creates a positive mindset. Why? Because you have to actively look for positive ways to reach out to help and support someone who is suffering or finding it difficult to cope. It gets you into a cycle of positive thinking and behaviour.

Kind gestures free you from focusing on yourself and enable you to reach out to someone else. You might want to organize your own way of helping other people: help a neighbour in need by picking up some shopping once a week, or offer to cut their grass.

If you know someone in need, offer to help them. Simply ask how you could help make a situation better.

You may feel you have little to offer, but whether it's a cup of tea, an invite to dinner or an offer to help carry something, it's thinking of and doing something for others that's important.

Reach out to someone you haven't talked to in a while. Do it today. Write them a card, email or text to let them know you were thinking about them. Ask how they are. Ask them about what's happening in their life – even if it's just to ask how their job, children, dog or health are. Just having to think about what you can enquire about shifts the focus away from yourself.

If you would like support and company when you help others, you can volunteer your time and help with a local community group.

'I tried different voluntary roles. The one that really worked for me was volunteering with Citizens Advice (www.citizensadvice.org.uk). It was professionally run, I got good training, it was structured and I was supported. I was using my brain and I really felt I was making a contribution.'

There's a wide range of things you can do – from helping out in a care home or hospice to working in a charity shop, to supporting adults to learn to read or getting involved in a community garden. As a volunteer you can make a vital contribution to any number of aspects of community life.

Try to find an activity that offers:

- A role relevant to your interests. It may be related to the environment, conservation, arts and music or perhaps families and children.
- An opportunity to use the skills you already have or one that provides training to learn new skills.
- The opportunity for regular helping: a couple of hours a week. Frequency of helping is important, because it's a regular opportunity to take the focus off yourself and your worries.

Find out about volunteering opportunities near to you by visiting your local volunteer centre or visiting a relevant website such as www.volunteering.org.uk.

If you're anxious about the first step to volunteering, you could ask a friend or family member to join you as a fellow helper.

How family and friends can help you

It would be helpful for you if your partner, another family member or friend could read this book too. If they simply want a quick and easy understanding and some tips on how to help, though, encourage them to read this last part of the book instead.

If someone is suffering from anxiety, it can distance them from other people. Not only is this a problem for them, but for family, friends and colleagues it can also be a difficult challenge.

> 'My partner became a prisoner of my fears and anxieties; I grew more and more dependent on him. I could only go anywhere if he came with me.'

If you have a friend or relative who experiences high levels of anxiety, think about how *you* feel when you are worried or anxious: what goes through your mind, how you physically feel and what you do – how you respond when you're anxious.

Reflecting on your experience of anxiety might help you to understand, to a limited extent, how they feel when they are going through a bad time. Don't assume, though, that your experience of being worried about something is the same as theirs. Avoid phrases such as, 'Oh, I know exactly how you feel'. Different things trigger anxiety in each of us, we all experience different levels of anxiety and we all think, feel and respond differently.

It's not easy to empathize with and understand someone else who is anxious or has an anxiety disorder, because it's so different from the normal anxieties that people experience in their everyday lives.

When, for example, someone has a panic attack, they can be overwhelmed with a feeling of imminent death or doom and experience intense physical symptoms including those that feel the same as a heart attack. They're not making it up. It feels very real. And it's scary.

So it's important not to dismiss or make fun of a person's anxiety or push them into situations that are too much for them. Do not negate how they feel by saying things like, 'Everything will be fine', or 'Don't worry about it, it's nothing'. You may think you're being helpful, but rather than engaging with how the other person feels, you are, in fact, dismissing their feelings and may actually make things worse.

Finding a balance between being supportive and enabling

You need to be supportive. Being supportive is a question of finding the right balance: understanding and accepting how the other person is feeling, but avoiding getting caught up in, accommodating and giving in to their anxiety.

While giving in to anxious requests can keep things calm in the short term, in the long run it feeds into the cycle of anxiety. If you continually give in to their anxieties, you are actually enabling the anxious person's behaviour.

In psychology and counselling, the word 'enabling' is used to describe a situation where one person responds – often with good intentions – to another in a way that perpetuates and even exacerbates another person's anxiety.

The enabler might do this by rescuing the anxious person from their predicaments. For example, in the case of a teenager who is anxious about coursework and exams, a parent might spend every evening revising with their teenager and more or less write their essays for them. Another example would be a man who declines social invitations and makes up excuses to friends so that his partner can avoid leaving the house and going out.

When you enable someone else's behaviour, you make accommodations for what they will or won't do and you bear the consequences for them. This means that firstly, the person themselves has little or no incentive to overcome their anxiety and secondly, it sends the message that there really *is* something to fear, which only fuels their anxiety.

So, although you are not to blame for their anxiety, you are responding in such a way that you are supporting their anxiety. It's a difficult situation; by opposing and challenging them they may retreat further into their anxiety. But by trying to pacify them, they can avoid doing anything at all.

How to help
What to do? Two things. First, you need to set some limits about what you will and will not make allowances for and get involved in. Setting limits is not always easy but it helps stop you being entangled in the other person's anxieties and fears and helps you to step back and think about how best you can support them.

Secondly, you will need to encourage them to overcome small challenges in order to manage their anxiety. In this way, they can build up their confidence and start to feel more in control.

Be clear what they are anxious about

Start by finding out what it is, exactly, that the other person is worried about. What do they think is going to happen?

Gently ask questions. Then summarize what they've said – what you understand to be the problem; how the anxious person perceives it.

Set limits: negotiate and compromise

Rather than dismiss or give in to their anxieties and fears, the best approach is to negotiate and agree a compromise. You'll need to help to identify one small step they could take.

For example, Ellie's mother Doreen belongs to a social club that meets once a week. Doreen has recently been diagnosed with cataracts and has been told not to drive until after an operation to remove the cataracts. The operation will be some months from now. She tells Ellie she still wants to go to the club but doesn't want to get the bus there and back. Doreen asks Ellie if *she* will take her each week.

Ellie says she does not want to commit to taking her Mum to the club and back each week and suggests Doreen phones another club member for a lift. Doreen says she's anxious about phoning someone for a lift in case they say no and then Doreen would feel very embarrassed.

From past experience, Ellie knows if she gives in, Doreen will find other situations when she needs Ellie to ferry her around. Instead, Ellie suggests that she either gets the bus to the club and back with Doreen next week, so that Doreen can get the bus on her own in future, or she gives her Mum a lift to the club next week and, together, they find out if there is someone else in the group who could give Doreen a lift each week.

Rather than take over the situation and rescue the anxious person or dismiss their feelings, it's important to work together to identify something that they can do – however small it is – towards managing an anxiety-provoking situation.

Give them a break from their worries and anxious thoughts: Do things together

It's important to give an anxious person time to talk about their situation and feelings, as well as helping them to overcome small challenges. However, it's also really helpful if you can do things together: something interesting, relaxing and/or fun.

'One thing that really helped me overcome the fear of going out as a result of panic attacks was agreeing to go out for short walks or to a café with my friend Cath, rather than stay in.

Cath helped me face my fears by taking things one thing at a time and although I sometimes felt very panicky, with her encouragement and reassurance, it gradually became easier and easier.'

As well as providing support and reassurance, finding ways to have fun is a positive thing you can do for them. I recently took a friend to see a comedic act called 'Fascinating Aida' – we both fell about with laughter and felt so good after the show. For the whole of the next day, we kept remembering the hilarious songs they performed.

Every person's experience of being worried and anxious is different, and each person has different needs. It's not always easy to know exactly what you should do, but here are some tips to help with this:

- If your friend, partner, family member or colleague has an anxiety disorder, do learn something about it. Read up on the different types of anxiety disorders. This will help you better understand. Chapter 2 of this book is a good start!
- Try not to assume you know what the other person feels or needs; it's best to ask or encourage them to talk to you about how they feel.
- *Do* let this person know that they can talk openly to you about their thoughts and feelings; that you aren't going to judge them or change the way you think or feel about them based on anything they say – even if they say the same fear over and over again (because, for many, the thoughts and fears are nearly always the same each time).
- *Do* let the other person know how and when they can call you. Knowing that someone is there to pick up can actually be reassuring and comforting to someone suffering with anxiety. Anxiety can make people feel lost and alone. Knowing that someone is a phone call away reduces that feeling.
- However, do set limits: tell them when you are not available and help them to identify other people they could phone or call upon – for example, other friends or a helpline.

- Try and a keep a normal routine, but be aware of the need to be flexible; know that sometimes the other person will have anxiety attacks and setbacks that will impact on *your* day.
- Reassure them that setbacks do occur, and that they shouldn't be disheartened if they have a bad day.
- Let the anxious person set the pace for recovery, but always encourage them to try and move forward.
- Be sure to praise achievements, no matter how small they seem.
- Be reliable: if you agree to be at a certain place at a specific time, be there or text or phone to let them know you'll be late.

Dealing with someone else's anxiety can often feel like dragging a piano up a hill: it's not easy and it can be exhausting. Anxiety can strain relationships and may cause you a lot of stress. You could even start getting anxious about the anxious person! Be sure that you have support and you take time out. Just as we are advised in the eventuality of an emergency on a plane to put on our oxygen mask first, you need to look after yourself so that you are more able to help someone else.

In a nutshell

- Voicing your worries can take away a lot of their scariness. If you can't talk to a partner, friend or family member, your doctor, a counsellor or a support group may help.
- You need positive people – 'radiators' – in your life; people who are more likely to respond to you in a positive way.

- Spend less time around people in your life who are 'drains' – those who take away your energy and resources, and where their negativity can increase your anxiety.
- Read about people who have coped with difficult times in their lives. Their stories can inspire you and help you to think along positive lines.
- Helping others frees you from focusing on yourself, which, in turn, can get you into a cycle of positive thinking and behaviour.
- It's important not to dismiss or make fun of a person's anxiety or push them into situations that are too much for them.
- Being supportive means that you try and understand and accept how the anxious person is feeling while at the same time avoiding getting caught up in, accommodating and giving in to their anxiety.
- Set some limits. Negotiate and compromise. Encourage the anxious person to overcome small challenges. In this way, they can build up their confidence and feel more in control.
- As well as listening and talking with them and helping them overcome small challenges, find some interesting, relaxing and/or fun things to do together.

Conclusion

'Without a doubt, I understand my anxiety better now that I know how and why my mind works the way it does. Knowing how my thought process works means I'm able to challenge it much more effectively.

I'm not completely free from the anxiety, but I feel like I have a handle on it; that I have a range of ways to deal with it.'

I hope that having read this book, you've got a clear idea of how anxiety 'works'. Hopefully, seeing anxiety in terms of thoughts, physical feelings and behaviour – and seeing how each aspect influences the other two – makes it easier to understand how and why anxiety can affect you.

I hope, too, that reading about other people's experiences of anxiety has helped you to realize you're not alone; there's nothing weird or unusual about you, your thoughts, feelings or behaviour.

I also hope that the advice, strategies, tips and techniques in this book are really going to help you manage and overcome anxiety.

Conclusion

Not every strategy works the same for every person and every experience. You might find that replacing negative thoughts with more realistic, positive thoughts is helpful. Or you might find that doesn't work for you, but acknowledging and accepting your thoughts is far more effective. You may find that one particular breathing technique works for you in some situations but not in others.

Try to identify and develop a range of strategies. Then you can pick the right strategy or technique for the right situation.

It might help if you were to make a 'Support Plan' which you could keep on your phone or written down on paper. It could include:

- A reminder to acknowledge and accept your thoughts;
- A reminder to be aware of negative thoughts, to challenge them and replace them with more positive thoughts;
- A reminder to BREATHE;
- The activities that help you to use up anxious energy;
- The activities that help to divert your thoughts and behaviour;
- Photos of things and places that help you feel calm;
- Names and contact details of supportive friends and family and contact details of professionals and support organizations.

Keep a look out for new ways – new approaches, strategies and techniques for managing anxiety – that could be helpful to you. If you can do this, not only will you have widened your range of strategies and techniques, but if, at any point, a particular approach no longer works for you, you can drop it and try one of the new ways.

Worry, anxiety and fear control you when you assume there's only *one* way to respond. But, with a handful of strategies, ideas and techniques to hand, you *do* have a choice and can do things to manage, and very often overcome, anxiety.

Take your time. You're going to need courage, persistence and determination. Sometimes you'll feel like you're really getting a grip; other times you might feel that you're wobbling. Acknowledge that and accept it.

If you manage to lessen or even overcome just one aspect or anxious issue, you're doing well. Remember, thinking and doing things differently is part of a process: a *series* of changes that happen to move you in the right direction. Change doesn't happen all in one go!

If, however, you feel your situation remains largely unchanged and you can't see yourself making progress, or you would like more help and support with the self-help strategies and techniques described in this book, do speak to your GP who can tell you about the other options available.

Good luck!

Other Useful Resources

Websites

Anxiety UK
www.anxietyuk.org.uk
Anxiety UK works to relieve and support those living with anxiety disorders by providing information, support and understanding via a range of services, including 1:1 therapy.

They can provide support and help if you've been diagnosed with, or suspect you may have, an anxiety condition. Anxiety UK can also help you deal with specific phobias such as a fear of spiders, blushing, vomiting, being alone, public speaking, heights or any fear that's stopped you from getting on with your life.

Mind
www.mind.org.uk
Mind provides information, advice and support to empower anyone experiencing a mental health problem.

British Association for Counselling & Psychotherapy (BACP)
www.itsgoodtotalk.org.uk/therapists
A directory of therapists provided by the British Association for Counselling and Psychotherapy (BACP) – a professional body representing counselling and psychotherapy.

Co-Counselling International
www.co-counselling.org.uk
Co-counselling is reciprocal peer counselling: co-counsellors take it in equal turns to be client and counsellor. Co-counsellors make their own arrangements to meet up, usually in pairs, for co-counselling sessions. Co-counselling sessions are free.

Helpguide.org
www.helpguide.org/home-pages/anxiety.htm
A US website that provides comprehensive information about anxiety.

The Samaritans
www.samaritans.org
Telephone helpline: 08457 90 90 90. The helpline is available 24 hours a day to provide confidential emotional support for people who are experiencing feelings of distress, despair or suicidal thoughts.

My other books

You might also find my other books helpful if you are struggling with anxiety:

- *The Mindfulness Colouring and Activity Book* (2016);
- *How to Deal with Difficult People* (2015);
- *Mindfulness Pocketbook* (2015);
- *Emotional Intelligence* (2014);
- *Mindfulness* (2013).

Books to help children overcome anxiety

- *The Huge Bag of Worries* by Virginia Ironside and Frank Rodgers (2011);
- *What to Do When You Worry Too Much: A kid's guide to overcoming anxiety* by Dawn Huenner and Bonnie Matthews (2005).

About the Author

Gill Hasson is a teacher, trainer and writer. She has 20 years' experience in the area of personal development. Her expertise is in the areas of confidence and self-esteem, communication skills, assertiveness and resilience.

Gill delivers teaching and training for educational organizations, voluntary and business organizations and the public sector.

Gill is the author of the bestselling *Mindfulness Pocketbook* (2015), *Mindfulness* (2013), *Emotional Intelligence* (2014), the *Sunday Times* bestseller *How to Deal with Difficult People* (2015), plus other books on the subjects of resilience, communication skills and assertiveness. Gill has also recently published *The Mindfulness Colouring and Activity Book* (2016).

Gill's particular interest and motivation is in helping people to realize their potential – to live their best life! You can contact Gill via her website www.gillhasson.co.uk or email her at gillhasson@btinternet.com.

Index

behaviour (*continued*)
  panic attacks 35–6
  phobias 37
  self-talk 60
  social phobia 39
beliefs 8, 52, 90
  believing in yourself 149
  changing your 67
  'shoulds' 55
best case scenario 131–2,
  135
beta blockers 112
black and white thinking
  54–5
blood pressure 18, 114
blurred vision 35, 40
body language 152–3, 155,
  160
books 142
brain 50, 56–7, 79, 82, 84,
  85, 128, 136
'brain-gut connection' 43–4
breathing 18, 19, 20, 22–3,
  24, 111
  agoraphobia 40
  breathing techniques 98,
    114–17, 120–1, 129,
    136, 152, 178
  exposure 138, 139
  generalized anxiety disorder
    33
  impact on physical
    symptoms 113, 121
  panic attacks 34–5
  phobias 37

bullying 25, 26
'butterflies' 19, 111

calming down 114
catastrophizing 53, 59
change 8, 179
  changing the way you
    think 77–84, 85
  physical symptoms 121
  stages of 78–9
chest pains 34–5, 36, 39
childhood experiences 25–6
chocolate 101
cigarettes 6, 7, 140–1
Cognitive Behavioural
  Therapy (CBT) 31, 73,
  140
cognitive defusion 100,
  102–3
cognitive distortions 53–6,
  57, 60–1, 67, 71, 97
cognitive fusion 21, 138
cognitive symptoms 8, 20–1
  agoraphobia 41
  generalized anxiety disorder
    33
  interaction with other
    symptoms 22–3, 24,
    26–7, 110
  irritable bowel syndrome
    44
  managing your breathing
    116
  OCD 42
  panic attacks 35

escape behaviours 126
exams 17–18, 20, 170–1
excitement 20, 44
exercise 5, 117–20, 121–2,
    142
'explanatory style' 56–7, 60,
    61
exposure 137–40, 145, 151

failure, fear of 21
faintness 34–5, 111
family
    advice from 133
    enabling 170–1
    generalized anxiety disorder
        32
    help from 9, 168–70
    influence of 25
    supportive 172–3, 174, 178
    talking to 163
    worries about 4, 5, 6
fear 17, 44, 89, 104, 151
    agoraphobia 40
    coping strategies 179
    of fear 36
    letting go 93
    physical symptoms 111
    social phobia 38
    triggered by memories 95
    writing down 93–4
'fight or flight' response 19,
    44, 111, 113, 117–18,
    121
films 142, 143
filtering 54

financial worries 4, 5, 32
'flow' 141, 144, 151
focus and engagement 90–1,
    95, 97, 101, 105, 141
food 120
friends 6, 16
    advice from 133
    help from 9, 168–70
    physical exercise with 119
    supportive 173–4, 178
    talking to 5, 163
fusion, cognitive 21, 138
future, worry about the
    89–90

games 142
generalized anxiety disorder
    (GAD) 32–4, 45
good things, noticing the
    81–2
Gordon, Bryony 82

habits 50–1, 57, 59
    changing your 77–8, 79,
        80
Hall, William James 3
happiness 166
headaches 7, 18, 24, 33, 109,
    111, 113
heart rate 18, 19, 20, 24, 110
    agoraphobia 40
    managing your breathing
        114, 115
    medication 112
    panic attacks 34, 35

Index

spirituality 143, 164
sports 142, 150
stomach problems 19, 22–3,
    25, 43–4, 109–10, 120–1
    see also digestive
    symptoms; irritable
    bowel syndrome
stress 26, 55, 111, 119
students 4, 5
support groups 163, 175
'Support Plan' 178
supportive, being 170–5, 176
surveys 4–6
sweating 18, 19, 24, 34–5,
    37, 39, 45
swimming 119, 142

Tai Chi 142
talking to someone 5, 94–5,
    163, 173, 174, 175
television 142, 143
thinking 49–61
    changing the way you
    think 67, 77–84, 85
    Cognitive Behavioural
    Therapy 73
    replacing negative with
    positive 67, 70–2, 74,
    84–5, 96, 178
    solution-focused problem
    solving 128–9
    see also negative thinking;
    positive thinking
'Thought Diary' 58–60, 71
thoughts 8, 20–1, 177

Acceptance and
    Commitment Therapy
    99, 100–1
agoraphobia 41
cognitive defusion 100,
    102–3
generalized anxiety disorder
    33
interaction with other
    symptoms 22–3, 24,
    26–7, 110
irritable bowel syndrome
    44
letting go 93, 98
managing your breathing
    115, 116
mindful approach 90, 91,
    92
OCD 41, 42
panic attacks 35
phobias 37
social phobia 39
solution-focused problem
    solving 128
writing down your 58–60,
    61, 71, 93–4
    see also negative thinking
tingling sensations 111, 113
tiredness 33, 112
trauma 25, 26
trembling 33, 35, 37, 40, 111
tunnel thinking 54, 57, 67

uncertainty 15, 104, 151
unemployment 5, 6

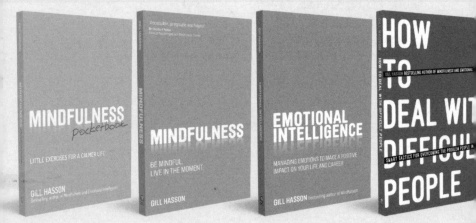